Image to Image
Volume I

by
Rita Carmack

Jewel Press

Image to Image—Volume I
ISBN 0-88144-047-7
Copyright © 1984 by Rita Carmack
Jewel Press
P.O. Box 2042
Windsor, CO 80550

Acknowledgements

I praise God for the inspirations from His Holy Spirit which enabled me to write this devotional book.

I also sincerely thank my daughter, Starlyn, and Wes Carmack for their editorial suggestions and proofreading. I thank Liz Webb for typing the manuscript and Kent Austin for the cover photo. And as always a special thanks to my husband, Derin, for his loving support of my writing.

Dedication

With deep love and appreciation I dedicate this book to my father. His love, dedication and faithfulness to God have been a goodly heritage.

"Alleluia! Happy is the man who fears Yahweh . . . Children of such a man will be powers on earth, descendants of the upright will always be blessed." (Psalms 112:1, 2, *Jerusalem Bible*)

Contents

Contents

Foreword

Affirmations are positive statements of what one desires to be done in his life through God and His Word.

Romans 4:17 states that God "calls things that are not as though they were" (*NIV*). That is what you do when you make affirmations based on God's Word. As you apply prayer and scripture with these affirmations of God's truth, they become reality in your life.

Never make an affirmation without quoting the scripture upon which it is based. Affirmation of God's Word is not an exercise in positive thinking and speaking. It is an exercise for *spiritual* healing and renewal. God's Word is to be kept before your eyes and in your heart to bring life and health to your *whole* body. (Prov. 4:20-22.)

These confessions are to be said aloud. Since "faith comes from hearing, and hearing by the word of Christ" (Rom. 10:17 *NAS*), you need to hear these words spoken audibly so they will be established in your spirit and will renew your mind. (Rom. 12:2.)

In these devotionals I will be giving you one or more affirmations per week to be said every day of that week. There are some you will need to say three to six weeks before you know they are established. Be free to review and repeat these statements whenever Satan comes against you in a weak area.

I have also provided scripture references from which you should choose at least three to quote in conjunction with your affirmation. This application of God's living Word is designed to be a part of your daily devotions. For faster results you can make these affirmations before you go to sleep at night and/or at various times during the day.

Each day review and repeat the affirmations given earlier in order to establish the renewal of your mind. Make each affirmation for at least three weeks (preferably for 40 days) or until you are free and established in the area in which you are confessing victory.

Continue repeating these confessions until you have won the victory in that area of your personal and spiritual life.

Don't become discouraged if you don't see immediate results in every instance. Some of these areas are more difficult to gain control over than others so you may not always be able to proceed at the same rate or with the same consistent degree of success. For years now I have been affirming health because it is my desire to always walk in divine health. Some affirmations I made only briefly, because the problem was taken care of very quickly, and I knew it. Other affirmations I make on occasion as I feel the need. For instance, I affirm strength whenever I am tired and am faced with a great deal of work I must get done. You will soon learn which are your problem areas, the ones requiring more intense concentration than the others.

Whatever your own personal situation, you must be assured that this approach to God's Word of promise will produce results — if conscientiously and faithfully applied. This book is not intended to be just another "nice little devotional," full of inspirational and uplifting thoughts and quotes from man, with a few Bible verses thrown in to make it appear "religious." This is a very practical "job manual" designed to literally change your life, to conform it to God's plan for you — to help transform you into His own image in spirit, mind and body.

Nor is it designed for easy reading. It is not my purpose to entertain. Rather, I want to see people's lives turned around, changed and healed through reading and applying the truths contained in these pages. I want to see our world transformed until it conforms to the image of God's own Son. (Rom. 8:29.) That transformation must begin with us Christians as individuals, then our families and then spread outward to encompass all those about us.

It is my prayer that God will bless you as you read and apply these truths to your life because you are committed enough to be a doer of the Word and not content to be a hearer only. May God bless you! I love you!

Here is my personal prayer for you:

"Heavenly Father, I ask that Your Holy Spirit will encourage, enlighten and enable the person who is reading this book.

"As he or she learns more about You and Your Word, may they grow strong in faith and knowledge, becoming more Christ-like each day.

"I pray that this book will bring healing to their spirit, mind and body that they may be completely whole and congruent in all areas of their life.

"In Jesus' Name, Amen."

Rita Carmack
October 1984

Week 1
Healing of Memories

Week 1 Day 1
Healing of Memories

"Then you will lift up your face without shame....
"You will surely forget your trouble....
"Life will be brighter than noonday....
"You will be secure, because there is hope."

Job 11:15-18 NIV

There are Christians who do not feel free and joyful because they are captive to the sins and sorrows of their past.

This week's devotionals will show you how to be set free in your subconscious mind and your spirit. (Some say the subconscious and the spirit are the same thing. Since I cannot prove this concept scripturally, I will not say it; however, it is obvious that the two are closely linked together because a person who has hurts in his subconscious is not free in his spirit.)

Proverbs 18:14 asks, "...a broken spirit who can bear?" (*NAS*). We human beings were not created with the mental or physical capacity to handle a broken spirit. We must give our brokenness to God and allow Him, through the sacrifice of Jesus and the power of the Holy Spirit, to heal us spiritually and set us free.

In my years of counseling and teaching I have had a "rude awakening" because of all the hurts and sorrows and sins people have shared with me. The depth of problems and despair in our world is truly overwhelming!

The only hope for our world is God, and He must have us Christians to work through. When we ourselves are hurting and unhealed, it is almost impossible for us to reach out and help others effectively.

My desire is that Christians become whole in spirit, mind and body. (I call this wholeness being a congruent

13

person.) When we are whole then the world can see, in us, that Jesus is the answer to their problems also. We can then touch others, showing them the way to true peace, joy, and freedom.

As you begin this study, read this prayer out loud in sincerity of heart:

Prayer: "Dear Father, I pray that as I read this devotional I will have the eyes of my heart enlightened to Your truth. Please flow through me and use me as a vessel to help Your children to be healed totally and to become completely free in their spirits.

"May I become so dynamic and confident and loving that people will see Jesus in me and know that He is their answer.

"In the powerful Name of Jesus I pray, Amen."

Today's Scripture Reading: Isaiah 49:8-18
*Affirmation: "All my past hurts are healed and my spirit is free because of the love and redemption of Jesus."

Affirmation Scriptures (Confess at least three of these daily): *Job 11:15-18; Psalm 30:11,12, 119:32, 147:3; Isaiah 61:1-3, 49:9,13, 43:18,19; Ezekiel 18:31; Hosea 11:3,4; Matthew 11:28-30.*

Week 1 Day 2
Healing of Memories (Infancy)

"...say to the captives, 'Come out,' and to those in darkness, 'Be free!' "

Isaiah 49:9 NIV

Satan comes to steal, kill and destroy. (John 10:10.) Part of his plan of destruction is to cause as many hurtful things as possible to happen to us very early in our lives so that he can use these against us later.

Satan is the one who makes a woman fearful as she carries an unborn child within her body. If there were no fear, the birth process would be much easier and some of the

---

*Please see Foreword for directions on how to use affirmations.

earliest "scars" in the subconscious mind would be eliminated.

The memories of our birth and babyhood are forgotten by our conscious mind, but our subconscious still carries any hurts, fears and/or anger that were encountered then.

Have you ever wondered why adopted children seem to have an above-average amount of problems? I believe it is because they sense rejection, probably even in their mother's womb, when she made the decision to give her baby up for adoption. Even though the mother's decision may have been made out of love, believing the child would have a better life in the adoptive home than she could provide herself, the possibility of hurt still remains strong. I am sure Satan says to that child as he or she is growing up: "Even your own mother didn't love you. She gave you away. She didn't want you." Such negative imput sets the child up for a sense of feeling unloved, rejected, unworthy.

Even in the best of homes, there are "unplanned" children whom Satan convinces were unwanted because they were a "surprise baby" or born late in the parents' life or were not the sex desired by the parents or were the last child born into a rather large family.

Satan uses any and all of the negative things that happen to us — even from the day of conception and during those early years that we don't remember.

The good news is that God does remember *everything*. Time is no barrier to Him. So through the power of the Holy Spirit, in God's infinite love, through the sacrifice of Jesus who truly "paid it all," all of these hidden hurts can be healed and we can be set free from them.

Prayer: "Dear Father, my conscious mind does not remember what happened to me as an unborn baby and in infancy, but You do. Please touch and heal my subconscious mind and my spirit from all fear, trauma and hurts that came into my life at that time. I yield my mind and heart up to You and fully expect the light of Your love

15

to bring healing and complete release. Please replace any feelings of rejection with the knowledge that I am loved and always have been, that Jesus has always been near me, loving me and longing to provide comfort, peace and joy to my spirit.

"Right now, I accept that comfort and love from You. Thank You for healing all the prenatal, birth and infancy hurts within me.

"In Jesus' Name, Amen."

Today's Scripture Reading: Psalm 139 (note especially verses 13-16)

Week 1 Day 3
Healing of Memories (Childhood)

...Jesus...said unto them, "Permit the children to come to Me; do not hinder them; for the kingdom of God belongs to such as these."

Mark 10:14 NAS

How it must have grieved Jesus to see the hindances that were in your childhood! All the time He was longing to reveal His love and care to you, but instead you had parents or other people in your life who used criticism, ridicule, angry words and/or physical abuse against you.

Now Jesus longs to heal all of that. But He cannot because you are still walking in unforgiveness and bitterness. No matter how hurtful your childhood was (and believe me, I have heard about some very sad ones!), God is able to take away those hurts.

The memory of the incidents will still be there, but that memory won't bring pain any more. It is very much like a physical injury. You get a cut on your hand. When it heals, there may still be a scar there, but the pain of the injury is gone.

As you pray, allow the love and light of God to flow in and through you, healing all the hurts of your early childhood.

Prayer: "Dear Lord, as an act of my will, I forgive and release all the hurts of my childhood. I forgive my parents, grandparents, brothers, sisters and everyone who hurt me in any way. I allow Your forgiveness to flow through me to them.

"Now, because Your love is free to flow through me, I say it is also healing my spirit. Please shine the healing light of Jesus into all the dark and hurtful areas of my childhood, both remembered and forgotten ones, and take out all anger, bitterness, fear and pain — setting me free in my heart.

"Thank You, Lord, for doing this for me.

"In Jesus' Name, Amen."

Today's Scripture Reading: Mark 10:13-16; Matthew 11:28-30

Week 1 Day 4
Healing of Memories (Adolescence)

"Forget the former things; do not dwell on the past. See, I am doing a new thing!"

Isaiah 43:18,19 NIV

For many people, adolescence is a difficult period of their life. There are many emotional and physical changes taking place during this time. Often conflicts with parents and authority figures increase. What friends think and say becomes very important. Adolescents often say and do things that are really against what their spirit believes.

Many times a spirit of rebellion comes into these youngsters causing them to do things that are damaging to their spirit, mind and body.

If this is your story — if you experimented with drinking, drugs, the occult, pornography and/or promiscuous sex during your teen years — you will need healing from those guilts and bad memories.

Probably you have regrets and have put yourself down because of the foolish things you did. You need to forgive and release yourself, again allowing God's love to heal and set you free.

17

Prayer: "Father, I repent of the sins of my adolescent years. I ask forgiveness for the rebellion I allowed to operate in my life. Right now, I rebuke the spirit of rebellion and command it to leave me. In its place I establish a spirit of obedience and discipleship.

"I ask You, Lord Jesus, to cleanse me from all sexual impurity. I pray that the energy of Your blood will flow from the top of my head to the soles of my feet, cleansing me from defilement inside and out. I establish purity and self-control in my life.

"I renounce Satan and all his demons and I say that no demonic or occult influence can remain in my life.

"I speak healing to my body from any harm done by alcohol or drugs. I speak cleansing to my bloodstream, nervous system and brain. Forgive me, Lord, for abusing my mind and body. Thank You for that forgiveness. I accept it.

"I now forgive and release myself of all mistakes, sins and foolish decisions made in my youth. I will no longer allow Satan to cause me to put myself down or to condemn myself for them.

"Thank You, Lord, for the blood of Jesus which erases all my past.

"In His precious Name, Amen."

Today's Scripture Reading: Isaiah 43:1-4,18,19,25

Week 1 Day 5
Healing of Memories (Marriage)

Who is among you who [reverently] fears the Lord, who obeys the voice of His servant, yet who walks in darkness and deep trouble and has no shining splendor [in his heart]? Let him rely on, trust and be confident in the name of the Lord, and let him lean upon and be supported by His God.

Isaiah 50:10 AMP

For several years now Satan has been doing his utmost to try to break up marriages. First, divorce became prevalent among non-Christians. Now there are far too many Christian marriages breaking up.

I could write an entire book on this subject alone, but will try to condense what I have to say on this subject to bottom-line basics. (There is a week of teaching on marriage later on in this devotional.)

What I would like for you to realize today is that your marriage can be healed, that the hurts can be forgiven, virtually forgotten and taken away.

When you walk in forgiveness, the blockage to your prayers being answered is removed; God's Holy Spirit has direct access to your mate.

Here is a special prayer for forgiveness to flow in your marriage. If possible, both you and your mate should pray this together and then expect new love and joy to be manifested in your marriage. To make it even more personal, as you pray this prayer, speak the name of your mate in the blanks provided:

Prayer: ''Father, I come to You in the Name of Jesus Your Son. I ask forgiveness for the times I have been selfish, unforgiving, inconsiderate and hostile in my marriage. (If you have been physically unfaithful in your marriage, ask forgiveness for that also.) **My actions of the past have wounded _____'s spirit and damaged the oneness that should be in our marriage. I repent of these acts and attitudes that have broken the faith of our marriage and I determine in my will to turn away from them.**

''From now on I will seek Your wisdom in our marriage. I will show consideration, compassion, love and forgiveness in our day-to-day relationship.

''Lord, I am now ready to forgive _____ for everything that he/she has ever done to hurt me in any way. I ask for Your divine forgiveness to flow through Jesus and then through me to _____. I forgive and release him/her right now. I rebuke and cancel all negative words I have ever spoken about _____ or our marriage. I say that those words can no longer operate against us or our home in any way.

"Father, I ask that You put a watch on my mouth that I never again say negative things against _____ or our marriage. I now bless _____ with the love and light of Christ. I bless our marriage with spiritual growth and with a spirit of love and forgiveness.

"I bless both of us, in Jesus' Name, with the assurance that we are loved and accepted by each other. I ask that the spirit of our marriage be totally healed and that we become truly one in You.

"I also pray that our marriage and home will be a witness to this hurting world of what God can do to give true love and joy in human relationships. I praise and thank You, Father, for blessing us and for giving us fulfillment in our marriage and home.

"In Christ's Name, Amen."

Today's Scripture Reading: Colossians 3:12-19; Ephesians 5:22-33

Week 1 Day 6
Healing of Memories (Marriage — con't)

Has not the Lord made them one? In flesh and spirit they are his....So guard yourself in your spirit, and do not break faith with the wife of your youth.

Malachi 2:15 NIV

Now that you have forgiven, you have cleared the way for God to heal your spirit from the hurts you have had in your marriage (or from divorce).

I am not naive. I know there are relationships which seem to be impossible to restore. But with God I know that they too can be changed.

Please don't put all the blame on your mate. In sincerity ask God to show you what areas you need to change in your marriage.

Wife, check to make sure you are not manipulative and nagging. Husband, make sure you are not being selfish and insensitive.

20

This is my prayer for you:

"Father, today I lift up this husband and wife who have been wounded in their spirits from the hurts in marriage. I ask that You help them yield these hurts up to You so that the blood of Jesus and the balm of the Holy Spirit can cleanse and heal all of them.

"I say that angry and hurtful words, swearing, physical abuse and sexual misuse are all being forgiven and healed.

"Thank You, Lord, that the light of Your love is flowing through this couple, taking away all darkness.

"I speak healing to the spirit of this marriage. I say it will now be founded on mutual love and respect.

"I bless both husband and wife with a spirit of love, consideration, compassion, understanding and cooperation with each other.

"Thank You, Lord, that the spirit of this marriage is strong in You.

"In Jesus' Name, Amen."

Today's Scripture Reading: Ephesians 5:21-33

Affirmation: "I have forgotten completely all past hurts and mistakes in my marriage. I have released _____ and I allow God's love to flow through me to him/her."

Affirmation Scriptures: Colossians 3:13; Ephesians 4:32; Proverbs 17:9; 1 Corinthians 13:4-8.

Week 1 Day 7
Healing of Memories (Releasing God)

"...it was I (God) who healed them. I led them with cords of human kindness, with ties of love; I lifted the yoke from their neck and bent down to feed them."

Hosea 11:3 NIV

Now that you have forgiven others, it is time to get rid of bitterness toward God. When things go wrong in life, people often ask my husband and me, "Why did God let that happen?" I have asked the same question myself. We know that God is all powerful and is certainly stronger than

Satan. Why then are so many people hurting? Why are there abused children, battered wives and disintegrating families?

The answer is simple. Bad things happen in life because God has chosen to limit Himself in the area of man's will, man's right to choose how he will live. If you were raised by abusive parents, that was not God's will. He provided redemption through Jesus, His Son, and He provided His Word for correction and teaching. Your parents had a choice to be Christ-like, patient, understanding and kind (and this is what God was longing for them to do!). Or they had the choice of going Satan's way, allowing anger and hostility to rule them.

God will not force anyone to become a Christian against his will. Nor will He force anyone to follow His statutes. But whatever a person's attitude or actions, God will always continue to love him and call him unto Himself. Whether that person responds to that call or not is his decision.

Also, now, after the wrong choices have already been made by your parents or other adults in your past, God offers you the same choice. You can continue in hatred and bitterness, because of your past (and perhaps become an abusive parent yourself). Or you can choose to accept God's forgiveness, cleansing and healing and in Him become a new creation — with all things made new for you!

I am not giving this advice glibly! I praise God many times over for the wonderful parents I had — parents who chose to walk in His ways and who were kind and understanding in their treatment of me.

Since I have begun counseling with hurting people, I've heard of childhoods that are almost unimaginable to me. Only through God could these negative and cruel parents be forgiven. They made the wrong choice. You may have suffered from such a situation in your childhood. But it need not be the case with your own children. You can end the ''curse of the generations'' now by making the right choice.

You can choose Christ's way of forgiveness and love, or you can choose Satan's way of unforgiveness and bitterness, and in turn bring up children who are hurt and confused. If you will pray today's prayer and let forgiveness

22

flow, using the affirmations given in this book, you can be healed in spirit, mind and body of your deep hurts and become a completely new creation.

(If you were blessed by having been brought up in a loving and caring home, praise God for it and use today's prayer time to intercede for those less fortunate — the alcoholics, drug addicts, homosexuals, child abusers, and wife beaters whose childhoods were so hurtful that they were never taught a better way. Pray that the spirits of such people will be drawn to God and His love and that they will determine in their hearts to choose His ways.)

Prayer: "Father, I come to You in Jesus' Name, and although I still may not have answers to all the questions I have asked over the years, I am choosing now to accept Your ways and to allow You to make me into a new creation for You.

"Lord, flow Your forgiveness through Jesus and through me to those who have hurt me, especially my parents (or guardians). **Father, I now realize that through all the fearful times, You were there, longing to help me, to comfort me, and to change my situation for the better. So, as an act of my will, I now ask You to remove all anger and bitterness toward You. I release You, Lord, and I will no longer resent You.**

"I praise and thank You for freedom and healing in my life.

"In Jesus' Name, Amen."

Today's Scripture: Psalm 107

Week 2
Renewing Your Mind
Week 2 Day 1
Forgiving Yourself

"You will surely forget your trouble, recalling it only as waters gone by."

Job 11:16 NIV

You have forgiven all other people. You have released God. Today you are going to forgive yourself so you can be free of regret about anything in your past life.

Satan likes to have us condemn ourselves, to put ourselves down and to continue to feel ashamed, embarrassed or guilty even after God has fully forgiven us.

Here are some things to remember that will help you in this area. When God forgives you of a certain sin, He completely erases it and forgets it. Therefore, if that sin comes before your mind again, you can know it is not God who is bringing up your past. Therefore, resist Satan and inform him, "As far as the east is from the west, so far has (God) removed (my) transgressions from (me)" (Ps. 103:12 NIV).

Even when you sin after having become a Christian, it is not God who condemns you and makes you feel guilty — it is Satan. Jesus does not condemn. He just says, "Let Me show you a better way."

First John 1:9 assures us, "If we confess our sins, (God) is faithful and just and will forgive us our sins and purify us from all unrighteousness" (*NIV*). When you realize you have sinned, immediately confess that sin. Ask forgiveness of God and He will abundantly pardon you and cleanse you of all unrighteousness.

Since God's Word is true, you can then forgive yourself, knowing you are once again righteous and pure in God's sight.

Prayer: "Father, I ask that Jesus' forgiveness flow from You to me for any and all mistakes and sins of my past life. I repent of my sins and turn away from them.

"I allow Jesus' forgiveness to flow through me to myself and I now forgive myself of all the mistakes and sins I've committed. I free myself from all self-condemnation and release myself to become the person You would have me be. Like the Psalmist, I realize that I am fearfully and wonderfully made and am created in Your image!

"Thank You, Father. I give You praise and glory. Amen."

Today's Scripture Reading: Job 11:13-19

Affirmation: "I forgive and love myself because God forgives and loves me unconditionally."

Affirmation Scriptures: Jeremiah 31:3; 1 John 1:9,3:1; Ephesians 3:17-19; Isaiah 40:11, 43:25; Psalm 119:32, 130:7, 139:13,14; Romans 8:1.

Week 2 Day 2
Renewing Your Mind

...to bestow on them a crown of beauty instead of ashes, the oil of gladness instead of mourning, and a garment of praise instead of a spirit of despair. They will be called oaks of righteousness, a planting of the Lord for the display of his splendor.

Isaiah 61:3 NIV

In the past you have experienced ashes (burned out dreams), mourning and despair. God desires that, instead, you receive a crown of beauty, the oil of gladness and a garment of praise.

God wants you to be as steadfast and immovable as an oak tree. He wants to display His splendor through you. How can this steadfastness become true in your life?

Step One has already been taken. You have allowed God to flow through you to remove all the "junk" of your past life.

Now I am going to explain Step Two, which is an *essential* one if you are to avoid slipping back into those old hurts, emotions, and habits of the past.

This second step involves what is spoken of in Romans 12:2 as "the renewing of your mind."

What you have been doing the past several days will have already done much to cleanse and heal your subconscious mind and/or your spirit. But in your conscious mind there remain attitudes, habits, and thought patterns which must be transformed or renewed.

The very best way to renew the mind is to consistently replace negative thought patterns with positive affirmations based on and linked with the Word of God.

(I have previously suggested three affirmations which you, hopefully, have already been repeating aloud daily — if not, begin today to renew your mind.)

Prayer: "Father, I thank You that You have healed my spirit and set me free from my past.

"I ask that You now give me the determination and the self-discipline to do my part in finding complete and permanent healing by renewing my mind in Your Word.

"I know that as I speak Your Word it will become alive and powerful in me and will accomplish what You desire for me.

"In Christ's Name, Amen."

Today's Scripture Reading: Isaiah 61

Week 2 Day 3
New Thought Patterns

...be transformed (changed) by the [entire] renewal of your mind — by its new ideals and its new attitude — so that you may prove...what is the good and acceptable and perfect will of God...
Romans 12:2 AMP

There are old-habit patterns of thinking that need to be replaced in your thought life. There are old feelings of the past that will have to be rooted out and replaced with God's hope, peace, joy and self-control.

Some of these thought patterns may go very quickly; others, especially those which Satan has been using against you for many years, will only be expelled by diligent application of the Word over a period of time.

Some people claim that a habit pattern can be successfully changed in three weeks. In my own case, I have repeated many of these affirmations for as long as 40 days, until they and the corresponding scriptures were memorized and ingrained in my spirit. A few of these affirmations I have continued to make for years. Others I use "as needed" for a day or two at a time. The scriptures I have memorized are my ammunition against the temptations of the devil. They are my "way of escape" spoken of in 1 Corinthians 10:13.

(If you are an ambitious sort of person, eager to grow and change quickly, your tendency may be to "overload" on affirmations. I suggest that you not use more than six at any one time.

Last week you started two affirmations. This week you added a third. Today you will add a fourth. After you have added two more and it comes time to add the seventh, drop one of the first six — the one you feel is most established in you. Those that are "dropped' can be used and reviewed as they are needed.

What I am endeavoring to do in these devotionals is to get you free and healed and whole in spirit, heart, mind and body. These first few days have been devoted to spiritual healing. Now you can work on renewing your mind and on controlling your body. Of course, there will be some overlapping and going back and forth in the 13 weeks in which you will be following these devotional guides. I suggest that you continue this program for a full year. I know you are going to be growing in the Lord as you consistently apply His holy Word to your life.)

Prayer: "Father, I ask that You renew my mind in Your ways. Remove old habits of negative thinking and feeling. Fill my mind and emotions with the fruit of Your Spirit of love, joy, peace, patience, kindness, goodness, faithfulness, gentleness and self-control. (Gal. 5:22,23 *NIV*.)

"I pledge myself to be faithful to renew my mind in Your Word, to study, meditate on and memorize the Holy

Scriptures. **Please make the Word come alive in my spirit, changing me from the inside out.**

"Thank You for helping me to rid myself of the old negatives and to be transformed into an accurate image of Jesus.

"In His Name, Amen."

Today's Scripture Reading: 2 Corinthians 3:7-18

Affirmation: "My attitudes and emotions are in God's control. I have the mind of Christ as I daily confess the Word of God."

Affirmation Scriptures (Look up and read these scriptures — preferably in *The Amplified Bible* — and choose three to use in your daily confessions): *Romans 8:6, 12:2; Philippians 4:8, 2:5; 1 Corinthians 2:16; 2 Corinthians 10:5, 3:18; Colossians 3:8-10; Proverbs 16:3.*

Week 2 Day 4
The Choice Is Yours

The mind controlled by the Spirit is life and peace.
Romans 8:6 NIV

The general public searches for life and peace, but they go about it backwards. Instead of allowing God's Spirit to heal and control their spirit and their mind, they look for life and peace through alcohol, drugs, special diets and psychocybernetics (mind control, goal setting), group therapy, yoga, meditation and Eastern-type religious exercises. None of these provide lasting peace and fulfillment.

Jesus Christ is our Healer. God's Word is our protection, the way to peace and stability. The Holy Spirit is the One who reveals truth to us, and it is truth which sets us free! (John 8:32.)

You can have God's Word so completely ingrained in your spirit that it immediately comes to your mind whenever Satan presents temptation. You can become so saturated with the Word of God that you even quote scripture in your dreams. When that happens, you really know it is engraved in your subconscious mind and your spirit.

There are two ways of thinking; God presents thoughts to your mind, and Satan does the same. The choice of which way you think is up to you.

Thoughts lead to attitudes, emotions, patterns of thinking, words, actions, habits. God's thoughts, drawn from His Word, lead to loving attitudes, controlled, correct emotions, joyful thought patterns, kind words and actions, and good habits. But, Satan's thoughts produce a negative way of thinking and living.

Psalm 7:14 presents a good illustration of where the thoughts lead that Satan presents: ''Behold, [the wicked man] conceives iniquity, and is pregnant with mischief, and gives birth to lies'' (*AMP*).

In speaking of temptation, St. Paul declares: ''...no temptation or trial has come to you that is beyond human resistance:...But God is faithful [to His Word and to His compassionate nature], and He [can be trusted] not to let you be tempted...beyond your ability and strength of resistance and power to endure, but with the temptation He will [always] also provide the way out...'' (1 Cor. 10:13 *AMP*).

Notice that Paul states that God is faithful to His Word. When you use that Word against any temptation, God backs it up, and you overcome the temptation.

Prayer: ''Father, 'I have hidden your word in my heart that I might not sin against you' (Ps. 119:11 *NIV*). May that Word come alive and permeate my spirit, mind and body until I am completely controlled in all areas of my life by the love and peace of God. Amen.''

Today's Scripture Reading: Romans 8

Week 2 Day 5
Taking Thoughts Captive

Casting down imaginations, and every high thing that exalteth itself against the knowledge of God...

2 Corinthians 10:5a

...take captive every thought to make it obedient to Christ.
2 Corinthians 10:5b NIV

We need to firmly establish in our spirit that anything which comes to our mind that is not in agreement with God's Word is what is called in the *King James Version* an "imagination" and needs to be "cast down."

Even many of the common cliches of today are contrary to God's Word. For example, we hear people say: "Seeing is believing." But the Word of God says: "Believing is seeing." ("*...believe* that you have received it, and it *will be* yours" (Mark 11:24 *NIV*).) Human beings say: "Tell it like it is." The Word of God says: "Tell it like God says it is." ("God...calls things that are not *as though* they were" (Rom. 4:17 *NIV*).) The world says: "Sticks and stones may break my bones, but words will never hurt me." The Word of God says: "Death and life are *in the power of the tongue...*" (Prov. 18:21 *AMP*).

Listen to the conversation around you; to the news as reported on radio and television. Read your newspaper and current magazines. Measure them against the absolute truth of God's Word. You will find that much of what you hear is based on man's ideas and humanistic principles. In fact, a large part of it represents nothing more than the viewpoint of the person who reports it. You should definitely ask God to help you discern truth from error as you read and hear the news reports (especially in matters relating to the situation in the Middle East).

Here are some rather startling statistics which may help you understand the importance of what I am saying: In 1982 a study was done of the Top 240, the elite corps of American news journalists. It was found that 85% of these people described themselves as either agnostic or atheistic. Most of them reported that they did not believe in God, did not attend church and never studied the Bible. Only 7% said they ever went to any church service.

The study further revealed that the viewpoint of the majority of the top American news journalists differed substantially from that of 70% of the American public. It was thus concluded that our national news media is not at all representative of the vast majority of the American people.

These statistics were presented in a speech by Hilton Sutton who warned Christians not to become programmed by the non-Christian bias of the national news media. He also encouraged Christians to pray that members of the media will be born again. We need Christian journalists who know the Bible and who will give us truth in their reporting.

Prayer: "Dear Lord, forgive me for being ignorant of Your truth. Help me to seek to know Your ways, to have true knowledge and wisdom as a very real part of my inner being. Help me to be so strong in my spirit that Satan can never deceive my mind in any area.

"I cast down any theory or reasoning that sets itself up against the true knowledge of God, and I establish right thinking and knowledge in my mind.

"Father, please convict our journalists and news people so they will come to know You and to understand the truth.

"In the wisdom of Jesus I pray, Amen."

Today's Scripture Reading: Proverbs 9:6-12

Affirmation: "As an act of my will, I place my spirit, heart, mind and body in God's control. I walk in knowledge and obedience to His Word."

Affirmation Scriptures: Proverbs 20:27 (AMP); Romans 8:1,5,6 (AMP); Galatians 5:16,25; 2 Corinthians 10:4,5; 1 Corinthians 6:19,20; Philippians 3:21; John 6:63.

Week 2 Day 6
Right Thinking

...whatever is true, whatever is noble, whatever is right, whatever is pure, whatever is lovely, whatever is admirable — if anything is excellent or praiseworthy — think about such things.

Philippians 4:8 NIV

Do you realize that there is more good news in the world than bad? That may not be the case everywhere, but certainly it is true here in our United States!

Every day there are good, noble people who volunteer help in hospitals and nursing homes. Any sizeable town has organizations dedicated to helping people — the Salvation Army, united funds, half-way houses, Meals-On-Wheels, etc.

There is beauty in our world — singing birds, blossoming flowers, flaming sunsets, soft rainbows and smiles on people's faces.

To a very large extent what you decide to ''see'' and think about can bring either joy or discontent to your life.

I know two ladies. One lost two of her children within a 6-month period, about 17 years ago. She is cheerful, loves the Lord and reaches out to help and cheer others. The other lady had a son who died over 20 years ago. She is bitter, angry and a very unhappy person. Both of these ladies made a choice about a hurt in their life. The first woman chose to keep her mind attuned to whatever is true, noble, right, pure, lovely, admirable, excellent and praiseworthy. In the latter case, Satan is still ''winning'' — even after twenty long years!

If we consistently apply today's verse, thinking always of the good in life and refusing to dwell on the bad, we will have the abundant life that Jesus came to give us.

Prayer: ''Heavenly Father, thoughts of You and Your Son Jesus are the most pure, lovely and excellent I can have. May my spirit and mind be concentrated on You, Your Word and Your loving mercy. May I see Your handiwork around me, for in the words of the hymnwriter truly 'This is my Father's world, He shines in all that's fair!'

''In the beautiful Name of Jesus, Amen.''

Today's Scripture Reading (Read this in The Amplified Bible if possible): Philippians 4:4-19

Week 2 Day 7
Single-Mindedness

Roll your works upon the Lord — commit and trust them wholly to Him; [He will cause your thoughts to become agreeable to His will, and] so shall your plans be established and succeed.

Proverbs 16:3 AMP

33

Before your thoughts can truly become agreeable to God's will, you must know what His will is!

The Apostle James talks about a double-minded man being unstable in all his ways and unable to receive from the Lord. (James 1:5-8.) I believe that when a person's mind and spirit (or conscious mind and subconcious mind) do not agree, that person is double-minded.

To become single-minded (so you can *wholly* trust the Lord), you need to spend enough time in God's Word to establish it first in your spirit and then in your mind.

One reason I urge you to repeat scripture aloud is to help you memorize it so that it becomes an automatic response to quote it when Satan presents temptation. The other reason is to establish faith (absolute knowledge of God's will and His ways). Romans 10:17 stresses that faith comes from hearing the Word of God.

Some contend that repeating of affirmations and scriptures is "vain repetition." But it isn't. It is not vain because we are repeating God's powerful Word of truth and statements that agree with it. And the truth is never vain. God's Word is true, He has promised us that He will watch over it to perform it, that it will not return to Him empty! (Is. 55:11.)

Today's verse is the key to success in any venture in life — turning over your plans and your work to the Lord in full commitment and trust. But this can only be done when you know and understand His love, His ways and His will for you.

Prayer: "Dear Lord, help me to seek and find Your ways through the application of Your Word in my daily life.

"Heal my spirit and renew my mind that I may be free to achieve the success You desire for me.

"In Jesus' Name, Amen."

Today's Scripture Reading: Psalm 119:1-27

Week 3
Receiving the Holy Spirit

Week 3 Day 1
The Holy Spirit: Who Is He?

"And I will ask the Father, and he will give you another Counselor to be with you forever — the Spirit of truth....he lives with you and will be in you."

John 14:16,17 NIV

As a Christian your ultimate goal should be to have your spiritual heart completely controlled by God's Spirit and then to put your flesh (mind and body) under the control of your spirit. To accomplish this will require an exercise in discipline and day-by-day obedience.

First, you will need to understand who the Holy Spirit of God is, and what He wants to do for you. You will need to let Him into your life, to allow the fruit of the Spirit to develop in you, to accept the gifts He desires to give you, and then to walk in the light of this knowledge.

God is a three-part being: God the Father, God the Son (Jesus Christ), and God the Spirit (Holy Ghost or Holy Spirit). It may help you to relate this concept to yourself. You too are made up of three parts: spirit, mind and body.

Jesus was sent into a human *body* so He could be offered as a perfect sacrifice for our sins, so we could walk in grace, redeemed by His blood.

When Christ was preparing His disciples for His bodily absence (when He would later ascend into heaven to sit at the right hand of God the Father), He told them that they did not need to grieve because He would send the Comforter (Holy Spirit) to them.

In fact, they were told to wait and not to leave Jerusalem until they had received the Holy Spirit who would give them inner power. Then they were to go out and be witnesses "to the ends of the earth" (Acts. 1:4,5,8).

Even though they had physically walked with Christ for three years, He still said they were not to go out to minister until they had received the Holy Spirit. Surely we, too, need Him before we can go and minister effectively!

Receiving the Holy Spirit is not difficult. The instructions are given in Luke 11:13.9 *(NIV)*: "If you then...know how to give good gifts to your children, how much more will your Father in heaven give the Holy Spirit to those who ask him!" "Ask and it shall be given to you . . ."

If you desire the Holy Spirit, pray this simple prayer:

Prayer: "Dear Father God, I desire Your Holy Spirit to be in me. I yield my heart and life to you and ask that You give me Your Holy Spirit right now. I receive Him into my life and thank You for answering my prayer. In Jesus' Name, Amen."

(If you meant this prayer from your heart, you now have God's Spirit in you, according to His Word.)

Today's Scripture Reading: John 14:15-27; 16:5-15

Affirmation: "I am filled with and baptized in the Holy Spirit and have the fruit and gifts of the Spirit in my life."

Affirmation Scriptures: Luke 11:13; John 14:26, 16:13; Galatians 5:22,23; 1 Corinthians 12:7-11; Acts 2:39 (AMP); Hebrews 2:4; 1 John 4:13 (Wuest).

Week 3 Day 2
Giving the Holy Spirit Control

"The Spirit gives life; the flesh counts for nothing. The words I have spoken to you are spirit and they are life."

John 6:63 NIV

Now that you have accepted the Holy Spirit into your life, you will begin to see changes take place inside yourself. God's Spirit reveals truth to your human spirit. To have your life in God's order, you must put the Holy Spirit in control.

This is done as an act of your will and in saying the words to establish it in your own spirit and heart.

We live in a sense-oriented world. These are some humanistic sayings we've heard many times: "Seeing is believing"; "If it feels good, do it"; "Do your own thing." This is not God's way. His Word says: "...believe that you have received it, and it will be yours" (Mark 11:24 *NIV*). Jesus said that one should "deny himself and take up his cross and follow me" (Matt. 16:24 *NIV*).

Here is the order I believe that God would have us follow: 1) Put His Spirit in control over our human spirit, and then, 2) place our mind and body in subjection to our spirit. That way, we will not be ruled by our attitudes, habits or fleshly appetites, but rather will walk in the way of the Spirit, allowing the fruit of the Spirit to come to maturity in us.

Prayer: "Dear Father, thank You for giving me Your Holy Spirit in my life. I now submit my spirit to Him and allow Him to have rule over me. I ask You to strengthen my spirit and bless it with wisdom. I put my mind and body under the control of my spirit. In Christ's Name, Amen."

Today's Scripture Reading: Romans 8:1-27

Week 3 Day 3
Fruit of the Spirit: Love

But the fruit of the Spirit is love, joy, peace, patience, kind-ness, goodness, faithfulness, gentleness and self-control....Since we live by the Spirit, let us keep in step with the Spirit.
Galatians 5:22,23,25 NIV

I believe that if the fruit of love — toward God, others and ourselves — were perfectly manifested in us all, then other fruits of the Spirit would automatically be present.

Love is "the more excellent way" of which the Apostle Paul writes in the thirteenth chapter of 1 Corinthians. It is the very character of God. Jesus said that it would be by love that the world would recognize His followers. (John 13:35.) Love was perfectly exemplified in Christ Jesus. Yet for us, as followers of Christ, it seems that love is the most difficult of all the fruit of the Spirit. Why is it we have so much trouble manifesting and maintaining a constant and consistent attitude of love toward others?

Too often unforgiveness and bitterness block our love. Anger and hatred rise up within us. What is the answer? Where shall we begin?

This is not merely another exposition exhorting you to ''love as Jesus loved.'' We have all heard numberless sermons on that topic already! What we need to know now is *how* to love as Christ loves. There is a way to attain this attitude of love.

First, repent of an unforgiving spirit. As an act of your will, allow forgiveness to flow, unconditionally, through you to everyone.

Secondly, through confession of God's Word and right affirmations, replace any unloving or unforgiving attitude or emotion with love and acceptance of others.

Finally, learn to *develop* love. This is best done by *acting* in a loving way — whether your flesh wants to or not. Remember, your spirit is in control now and you can say and do loving things whether you ''feel'' like it at that moment or not.

Say kind (not negative or harsh) words to your family each day. Volunteer time on a regular basis to an organization which helps others (a hospital or nursing home, for example). Through some reliable organization such as World Vision, ''adopt'' one of the hurting children of the world and support him or her regularly through your gifts and prayers. Find a lonely older person in your church and offer transportation, companionship and home-cooked meals as often as you can. Put this Bible verse into effect in your life: ''...love your enemies, do good to them, and lend to them without expecting to get anything back. Then your reward will be great, and you will be sons of the Most High, because he is kind to the ungrateful and wicked'' (Luke 6:35 *NIV*).

Prayer: ''Father, I repent of the lack of love and forgiveness that has characterized my life. I ask You to forgive me. As an act of my will, I allow Your forgiveness and love to flow through me to everyone. I release any resentment I have

held against anyone and I ask to be filled with Your perfect love. Thank You that this is possible because of Your Son, Christ Jesus.

"In His Name, Amen."

Today's Scripture Reading: John 15:12-17

Affirmation: "I have a loving and forgiving attitude toward everyone."

Affirmation Scriptures: Ephesians 4:32; 1 Corinthians 13:4,5; Luke 6:28; 1 John 4:20; 1 Thessalonians 3:12; 1 Peter 4:8, 1:22.

Week 3 Day 4
Fruit of the Spirit: Joy

You turned my wailing into dancing; you removed my sackcloth and clothed me with joy, that my heart may sing to you and not be silent.

Psalm 30:11,12 NIV

Most people in this world are seeking happiness, but few seem to realize that what they really need is the spiritual quality of joy. Happiness is a fleeting thing which depends on the actions and attitudes of others and the circumstances of life. Joy comes from God; it enters the inner being and remains there in all of life's situations as God's Spirit ministers to the person's spirit.

Joy is the opposite of depression. The answer to depression is not taking "uppers," going on exciting trips, buying new clothes or cars, or finding a new marriage partner. These things only bring temporary relief from depression, if indeed they relieve it at all.

The real cure for depression is to replace it with a joy that cannot be destroyed by anything life brings. This kind of joy can only be received by allowing God's Holy Spirit to come into your heart and then by confessing with your mouth that you have joy. Joy comes when you truly beggin to understand the character of God — that He is the giver of every good and perfect gift. (James 1:17.) He is the One who always loves you unconditionally.

Prayer: "Father, I thank You that You replace my depression with joy. I ask that Your Holy Spirit fill me with Your joy at all times. Thank You for Your unconditional love and for Your gift of Jesus.

"In His Name I pray, Amen."

Today's Scripture Reading: John 15:5-11

Affirmation: "I have the joy of the Lord in my everyday life."

Affirmation Scriptures: Psalm 5:11, 16:11, 19:8, 97:11, 105:3; Isaiah 51:11; John 16:24, 17:13; 1 Peter 1:8.

Week 3 Day 5
Fruit of the Spirit: Peace

The fruit of righteousness will be peace; the effect of righteousness will be quietness and confidence forever.
Isaiah 32:17 NIV

Each year in our nation several million dollars are spent for tranquilizers and sleeping pills. Why? Because most people are not at peace with themselves! Many people, even Christians, are merely coping with life, not being overcomers.

Some time ago a local church held a series of Wednesday night meetings to discuss this topic: "How to Help the Christian *Cope*." And the advertisements for the meetings even said that "coping" was Biblical! I have a huge *Strong's Exhaustive Concordance of the Bible* which lists every single word in the entire *King James Version* (including every "and" and "the"). I looked through it for the word "cope." It isn't there!

As Christians we are not merely to cope. We are to overcome all circumstances of life through the application of the Word of God and the power of the Holy Spirit!

Coping will not bring inner peace. One of the names of Jesus is "the Prince of Peace" (Is. 9:6). Peace is one of the main themes of the Bible. We Christians are to be peacemakers here on earth!

To be a peacemaker, one must first have God's peace within himself. How is this achieved?

The first step, of course, is to be born again, to accept Jesus Christ as Lord and Savior.

Secondly, a person must receive the Holy Spirit and yield his life to Him, for the Bible says, ''...the mind controlled by the Spirit is life and peace'' (Rom. 8:6 *NIV*).

Thirdly, one must agree with God's Word concerning peace in his own life.

In John 14:27, Jesus says that He gives His peace to us. To have peace in your own life, accept and agree with His words.

Prayer: ''Dear Lord, I accept the peace You have provided for me through Jesus. I open my heart to allow a deep quiet calm to flow through my whole being. Your ways are peaceable. I will walk in them. Thank You, Father, for peace in my own heart; may it spread to my family, friends and even the whole world.

''In Christ's Name, Amen.''

Today's Scripture Reading: Isaiah 32:15-18

Affirmation: ''Christ's peace is within me giving me a calm and quiet spirit.''

Affirmation Scriptures: Psalm 94:19 (TLB); Proverbs 14:30 (NAS); Matthew 11:28-30; John 14:27, 16:33; Romans 8:6; Colossians 3:15; 2 Thessalonians 3:16.

Week 3 Day 6
Fruit of the Spirit:
Patience, Kindness, Gentleness

Therefore, as God's chosen people, holy and dearly loved, clothe yourselves with compassion, kindness, humility, gentleness and patience.

Colossians 3:12 NIV

I was blessed by God to be brought up by a mother who was patient, kind and gentle. Our relationship was one of love, peace and joy. I can never remember having a "fight" with my mother. Her spirit was so beautiful that even as a teenager, my response was love. I was filled with a desire to please my mother, never to hurt her.

What a different place this world would be if every child had the kind of example to follow that I had! Wars would cease and there would be peace, lasting peace.

My mother seemed to possess these qualities of patience, kindness and gentleness as a natural part of her personality. Most of us don't. However, through the power of the Holy Spirit, they can become a part of us. They will be the fruit of our spirit when that spirit is completely under the control of God's Holy Spirit.

You will develop these qualities in your own life by consciously yielding to the Holy Spirit and by agreeing with the Word of God.

Prayer: "Father, I praise You that Your Holy Spirit lives within me and controls my spirit. I thank You that I possess patience, kindness and gentleness in increasing measure in my life.

"In Jesus' Name, Amen."

Today's Scripture Reading: Ephesians 4:25-32

Affirmation: "God's Holy Spirit controls my human spirit so that I am patient, kind and gentle."

Affirmation Scriptures: Proverbs 14:29, 19:11; Galatians 5:22,23; 1 Thessalonians 2:7; 2 Timothy 2:24,25; Ephesians 4:2,3,29-32.

Week 3 Day 7
Fruit of the Spirit: Faithfulness, Goodness

"...Well done, good and faithful servant! You have been faithful with a few things; I will put you in charge of many things. Come and share in your master's happiness!"

Matthew 25:21 NIV

Goodness and faithfulness go hand in hand. Those who are faithful to God and His Word are good, trustworthy people. They do good for others and for themselves.

The world needs more faithful people. Talk to the owners of businesses. One of their major problems is apt to be employees who are not loyal and faithful, employees who are not dedicated to doing a good job for their company. Such people are often tardy or absent from work. If not constantly watched, they do not put forth much effort.

Some Christians are like that. They are not faithful in Bible reading and prayer. They are late for church services or miss them entirely. They do not support their church with their tithes. They cannot be depended upon to take care of the Lord's business.

If you are this kind of person, God desires to show you a better way! You can become a disciplined and faithful person by putting your mind and your body under the control of your spirit — which, in turn, is controlled by the Holy Spirit.

As an act of your will, make your body get up an hour earlier so you can have time for personal devotions each day. Commit yourself to going to church regularly. Give the Lord the tithe (10%) of all your income.

(I know some enlightened Christians who tithe in advance, by faith. Each month they give 10% of what they expect to receive in income the *following* month! More about this in the week on financial matters.)

Prayer: ''Father, I repent and turn away from unfaithfulness. As an act of my will, I put my spirit, mind and body under Your control and pledge to be faithful in Your service.

''In Jesus' Name, Amen.''

Today's Scripture Reading: Matthew 25:14-46

Affirmation: ''I am a good and faithful child of God.''

Affirmation Scriptures: 1 Corinthians 4:2; Ephesians 5:8,9; 2 Peter 1:5-7.

Week 4
The Gifts of the Holy Spirit

Week 4 Day 1
The Holy Spirit: His Gifts

Now about the spiritual gifts (the special endowments of supernatural energy), brethren, I do not want you to be misinformed.

1 Corinthians 12:1 AMP

I am in agreement with Paul. I do not want you to be misinformed (or "ignorant" as the *King James Version* puts it) about the gifts of the Spirit. This is probably the most misunderstood subject in the entire New Testament. Without a doubt it is one that is often taught incorrectly by today's Church (if not ignored entirely!).

According to Paul, the gifts of the Spirit are to be desired: "...desire earnestly spiritual gifts..." (1 Cor. 14:1 *NAS*). Why does Paul say this? Why should these gifts be so earnestly desired? Because it is by them that the power of the Holy Spirit is demonstrated. When correctly used, these gifts accomplish three things:

1. They draw non-believers to God. (1 Cor. 14:22-25.)

2. They build up the Church. (1 Cor. 14:4,12.)

3. They build up the person who possesses them. (1 Cor. 14:4.)

If all nine of the gifts of the Spirit were being evidenced in each local church body and used consistently by its congregation, there would be a tremendous drawing power to attract worldly people to come to church and be saved.

The gifts of wisdom, knowledge and discernment of spirits are to be used to help people minister to the emotional hurts and spiritual needs of others. These gifts also help to keep Christians from being deceived by Satan.

The gifts of healing, faith and miracles are to be used to meet the physical needs of the congregation. Jesus often used these gifts in His own personal ministry.

The utterance gifts — prophecy, tongues and interpretation of tongues — are used for encouragement and building up of the believers and to bring non-believers into a knowledge of the Lord.

How different, how alive, how vital our churches would be if God's children would desire and receive and operate in the gifts of the Spirit! Our churches would become centers of healing for spirits, minds and bodies. They would have great ''charisma,'' or drawing power, to attract people to Christ.

Prayer: ''Dear Father, I open my spirit, heart, and mind to Your Holy Spirit. I desire to have the gifts of the Holy Spirit in my life. Please give me the gifts You desire me to have, and help me to use them to further Your kingdom here on earth.

''In Jesus' Name, Amen.''

Today's Scripture Reading: 1 Corinthians 12

Week 4 Day 2
The Gifts Are For You

But to each one is given the manifestation of the (Holy) Spirit — that is, the evidence, the spiritual illumination of the Spirit — for good and profit.

1 Corinthians 12:7 AMP

Which of the gifts are operating in your life? If there are none, you should be finding out why, because according to this verse *each one* (each believer) is given a manifestation of the Spirit.

The gifts of the Spirit are so clearly taught in Chapters 12 and 14 of 1 Corinthians that it is difficult to understand how they have been so neglected by our churches today.

I praise God that almost five years ago I gave up my fears, opened myself up to teaching that was new to me, and prayed that God would give me, through His Holy

Spirit, the gift or gifts He knew I needed for my own spiritual growth and for the ministry into which He had called me and my husband.

Since then, there have been manifested in me, at one time or another, all nine of the gifts of the Spirit (with the exception of interpretation of tongues). The gift I use most often is that of praying in tongues. What a joy it is to be able to allow the Holy Spirit to pray to the Father through me by simply yielding my mind and tongue to Him. It certainly is more comforting and much more effective than my "Lord,-You-know-what-is-best" prayers of the past!

If your church background is similar to mine, this week's teaching on the gifts of the Spirit may be difficult for you to accept. I understand your doubt and hesitancy. I felt the same way. However, I would really challenge you to check out for yourself what I am presenting here. Search the scriptures to see what the Spirit reveals to you personally about this vital subject. Be open to receive whatever truth He shows you — and whatever gift or gifts He desires to give you.

Prayer: "Dear Lord, I pray that I may be able to let go of any false teaching from the past and allow You to reveal Your truth to me about Your Holy Spirit and His gifts. May the eyes of my spiritual heart be enlightened that I may be able to receive all You have for me in the Spirit-controlled walk. I desire to know the truth and to be set free through it.

"In the Name of Jesus, who promised to send the Holy Spirit to us, Amen."

Today's Scripture Reading: John 14:15-27

Week 4 Day 3
Revelation Gifts

To one is given in and through the (Holy) Spirit [the power to speak] a message of wisdom, and to another [the power to express] a word of knowledge and understanding according to the same (Holy) Spirit;

...to another the ability to discern and distinguish between [the utterances of true] spirits [and false ones]...
1 Corinthians 12:8,10 AMP

The gifts of the word (or message) of wisdom and knowledge and the discernment of spirits are revelation gifts. Perhaps I can best explain them with this illustration:

One evening a friend came to see my husband and me bringing with her a friend she wanted us to meet. My husband, Derin, had never met John* before.

As we visited, it was obvious that John had some serious hurts from his past life. All of a sudden Derin asked him, ''What does a military shovel and a dog have to do with you?''

Immediately John started sobbing and crying. When he could talk again, he told us that when he was a small boy his dog had been run over and killed. His stepfather, who was a military man, went and got his shovel and dug a hole in the back yard. John, being only a child, hung onto his dog because he didn't want it buried. The stepfather became very angry, hit John with the shovel and threatened to bury him also.

Then John went on to relate other very cruel things the stepfather had done to him during his childhood.

Later, John's mother sent him to live with his real father. For many years John had felt that his mother had rejected him, and he resented her for it.

Now, through recalling these past incidents, John realized that his mother had been acting in love by sending him to live with his father. She had felt he would be happier and better off if he were no longer subjected to the cruelty of his stepfather.

As this realization dawned upon John, he was able to forgive his mother. Soon afterward he went to see her and they were reconciled.

The word of knowledge Derin received was about the shovel and the dog. The word of wisdom was that which we used as we prayed for John, removing all bitterness, hurt

All names in this book have been changed to protect privacy

and resentment. These revelation gifts are invaluable in counseling, as they help us to get quickly to the root of people's problems. The gift of discernment alerts us when someone is trying to deceive us.

All these revelation gifts are available to you through the Holy Spirit of God.

Prayer: "Dear Father, thank You for Your gifts to us through the Holy Spirit. Please help me to have wisdom and understanding in receiving and using them in my life.

"In Jesus' Name, Amen."

Today's Scripture Reading: James 1:5-25, 3:13-18

Week 4 Day 4
Ministry Gifts

To another (wonder-working) faith by the same (Holy) Spirit, to another the extraordinary powers of healing by the one Spirit;

To another the working of miracles...

1 Corinthians 12:9,10 AMP

These gifts — faith, healing and miracles — are referred to as ministry gifts. Once again, these seem to be mostly used for helping others. Jesus used them often in His ministry. They served as proof that He was the Messiah, the Son of God. (Luke 7:18-23.)

In John 14:12, Jesus made this statement: "Verily, verily, I say unto you, He that believeth on me, the works that I do shall he do also; and greater works than these shall he do; because I go unto my Father." Then in John 16:7 He said that He was going to the Father so the Holy Spirit could be sent to the believers. It is this Holy Spirit who enables us to have and use the power and gifts in our lives to do all these things of which Jesus spoke.

The question is: As a believer in Jesus Christ are *you* doing the works that Jesus did, and even greater works than His? If not, why not?

If you haven't been doing these works, don't condemn yourself. Rather, take careful inventory of your spiritual life.

Ask God to reveal to you what it is you need to do to have the faith, healing and miracle power that Jesus had.

Matthew 5:16 states that men are to see our good works and glorify our Father in heaven. Most of us Christians don't display enough good works that glorify God. Certainly not the kind of works that Jesus did — much less greater works than His!

If all born-again believers would really begin operating daily in the fruit and gifts of the Spirit, the world would soon be won to Christ!

I plead with you to be open and receptive to the gifts that the Holy Spirit has for you so you can walk in power and authority as Christ did.

Prayer: "Dear Father, I am convicted that I have not had enough of Your power and wisdom in me to do the same works that Jesus did (let alone greater works!). Forgive me for not walking in Your ways as I should have. Please open the eyes of my spirit and heart that I may know the power of Your Holy Spirit. Help me to let this power flow through me so that I may see Your kingdom come and Your will done on earth as it is in heaven.

"In the powerful Name of Jesus, Amen."

Today's Scripture Reading: John 14

Week 4 Day 5
Vocal Gifts

...to another prophetic insight — that is, the gift of interpreting the divine will and purpose;...to another various kinds of [unknown] tongues, to another the ability to interpret [such] tongues.

1 Corinthians 12:10 AMP

These three gifts — prophecy, tongues and interpretation of tongues — are called the utterance or voiced gifts. Tongues and their use have been much maligned, I feel, by both sides (those for and those against them).

There are those who say, "If you don't speak in tongues, the Holy Spirit is not dwelling in you." Others

50

say that speaking in tongues is "of the devil" and/or unacceptable in their church. In my opinion, both of these viewpoints are wrong.

If you are from either of these two "traditional camps," I beseech you to pray that the eyes of your heart will be enlightened as you read the following scriptures!

"If you then, though you are evil, know how to give good gifts to your children, how much more will your Father in heaven give the Holy Spirit to those who ask him!" (Luke 11:13 *NIV*). Luke 11:9 says: "Ask and it shall be given to you..." (*NIV*).

Notice that there is no postscript here stipulating that a person who receives the Holy Spirit will automatically or immediately speak in tongues. The Holy Spirit can be within a person's spirit, yet not be in *complete* control of his body and tongue, or even his mind.

Derin and I have met many people who, having been taught against tongues, have a mental block against them. They receive the Holy Spirit when they ask Him to come in, but it takes time for them to learn to allow the language of the Spirit to flow from their spirit, past their mental blockage and out of their mouth.

First Corinthians 14:39 (*AMP*) says: "...do not forbid or hinder speaking in [unknown] tongues." This needs no explanation. It is perfectly clear. In view of this verse, it is difficult to understand why some Bible-believing churches forbid tongues.

In verse 18 of the same chapter Paul writes: "I thank God that I speak in [strange] languages more than any of you or all of you put together." Now if tongues are of the devil, why would Paul, an apostle of Jesus Christ and author of two-thirds of the New Testament, be thanking God for them?

I believe I have presented truth in this teaching. Please give it your prayerful consideration.

Prayer: "Dear Lord Jesus, please open my heart to receive what You have for me. I know You went to heaven to send me the Holy Spirit. If, because of ignorance or false

teaching, I have been missing any part of what I should have in my life, I ask You to reveal it to me. Give me the courage to walk in the light You give me.

"In Your Name I pray, Amen."

Today's Scripture Reading: 1 Corinthians 14

Week 4 Day 6
The Gift of Tongues

He who speaks in a tongue edifies himself...
I would like every one of you to speak in tongues...
Tongues, then, are a sign...for unbelievers...
1 Corinthians 14:4,5,22 NIV

To understand everything Paul is saying about tongues in 1 Corinthians 14, you need to read it with this thought in mind: Part of the time he is writing about the use of tongues *privately*, and part of the time about their use *publicly*. Unless this distinction is kept clear, you can become confused about Paul's teaching on tongues.

As a prayer language in private devotions, tongues need no interpretation. Spoken in public worship services, tongues should be interpreted so the hearers will be built up and encouraged by them.

In this chapter, Paul also states that he would rather the believers prophesy than speak in tongues. (v. 5.) Here he is speaking in regard to public worship. That fact is made clear by reading verses 18 and 19 in which Paul says that he is thankful he speaks in tongues more than his readers, but that *in church* he would much rather speak words that instruct people.

In verse 14 and 15 Paul writes of praying and singing with his *spirit* and with his *mind*. If these are one and the same, why would he mention both? When I pray with my spirit, it is in tongues; when I pray with my mind (which I subject to God's Spirit), it is in my own native language. The same is true of singing.

The advantage then of praying in the spirit — in tongues — is that you allow the Holy Spirit to pray *through* you, without mental blocks. Mentally, you may be unsure of how to pray correctly. You simply may not know how you should pray, what God's perfect will is in the situation. But certainly the Spirit knows God's perfect will; so as you allow His words to flow through you, you always pray God's will.

Prayer: "Dear Heavenly Father, I open up my spirit, heart, mind and body to be the temple of Your Holy Spirit. I want to be wholly filled with and baptized (immersed) in Your Spirit. Right now I yield myself (and loose my tongue) to be used of You as You will.

"In Jesus' Name, Amen."

Today's Scripture Reading: 1 Corinthians 14

Week 4 Day 7
Danger of Rejection of Tongues

It is written in the Law, By men of strange languages and by the lips of foreigners will I speak to this people, and not even then will they listen to Me, says the Lord.

1 Corinthians 14:21 AMP

This verse contains a quotation of Isaiah 28:11,12. It reveals that tongues were prophesied in the Old Testament. Before rejecting the teachings concerning tongues in 1 Corinthians 12 and 14, it would be wise to read and carefully consider what Isaiah 28 has to say about those who refuse to listen when God endeavors to teach them knowledge.

Isaiah 28:9 speaks of people being like babies, just weaned. In 1 Corinthians 14:20 Paul admonishes us: "Brethren, do not be children (immature) in your thinking" (*AMP*).

For years I was a member of a church which had lots of rules, but almost no power. Time after time I saw tragedy, heartbreak and defeat in the lives of the members of that church (all of them good and sincere Christians). Because of what I saw, I questioned God, asking Him why He allowed such things to happen to those who love and serve Him.

Then one evening I read Isaiah 28 and received my answer. Verses 9 through 13 of that chapter describe what is happening in many evangelical churches which have rejected the gift of tongues: "Therefore the word of the Lord will be to them [merely monotonous repeatings of] precept upon precept, precept upon precept; rule upon rule, rule upon rule; here a little, there a little; that they may go, and fall backward, and be broken, and snared, and taken" (AMP).

Churches which deny or refuse the gifts of God's Holy Spirit are often immature; they teach precept upon precept, rule upon rule. The Lord has endeavored to teach them by men who speak in other tongues, but still they have not listened. God says of such churches: "...my people are destroyed from *lack of knowledge*..." (Hosea 4:6 NIV).

That was the answer to my question, "Lord, why do these things happen to Your people?"

I remember a friend of mine, a pastor's wife, who was telling me how her husband's church "got rid of" those members who spoke in tongues. She made light of their "strange" beliefs. Since then, tragedy has come into her life in many ways. I do not mean to imply that it was sent by God, but without the power and gifts of the Holy Spirit a Christian is not fully prepared to withstand the attacks of the enemy. That should be a sober warning to all of us.

Prayer: "Dear Heavenly Father, please help me to be mature in my walk with You. Help me to live by the dictates of Your Holy Spirit, to walk above the plodding grind of precept upon precept, rule upon rule. Instead, enable me by the power of Your Holy Spirit to go on to the glory of the image of Your very likeness and to increase in power and authority until I am fitted to rule and reign here on earth in Your kingdom.

"Bestow on me every good and perfect gift that You have for me, enabling me to see and know that truly the kingdom of God is within me.

"In Jesus' powerful Name, Amen."

Today's Scripture Reading: Isaiah 28:9-29

Week 5
Your Self-Concept

Week 5 Day 1
Self-Acceptance

How great is the love the Father has lavished on us, that we should be called the children of God.

1 John 3:1 NIV

A very common problem among Christians is lack of a good self-concept. Before we can adequately love God and others, we must learn self-acceptance and self-love.

God's Word assures us of His love toward us. If God deems us worthy of love, then we *are* worthy. And God *does* love us, as His Word points out again and again: "I have loved you with loving-kindness" (Jer. 31:3 *NIV*). "He tends his flock like a shepherd: He gathers his lambs in his arms and carries them close to his heart" (Is. 40:11 *NIV*).

As you make your affirmation on forgiving and loving yourself (Week 2 Day 1) and repeat the above scriptures with that affirmation, you will begin to develop the kind of self-concept that God wants you to have, one which agrees with His Word.

That Word says that you are "the righteousness of God" (through Jesus Christ), that you are "complete in him" (2 Cor. 5:21; Col. 2:10). Since this is the way God sees you, how can you consider yourself inferior? You are not inferior! You can overcome feelings of inferiority through positive affirmation and confession of (agreement with) God's Word.

I think it is best to praise God while you affirm His Word. That way you make the scriptures personal as you confess them. Here is an example of how to make your "self-love" affirmation, with the corresponding scriptures:

"Father, I praise You that I can forgive myself and love myself unconditionally because of Your unconditional love and forgiveness.

"Thank You, Lord, for Your great love that is lavished upon me, that I am called a child of God. (1 John 3:1.)

"I praise You, Lord, that You have loved me with an everlasting love and have drawn me with loving-kindness. (Jer. 31:3.) Thank You for being my shepherd and carrying me close to Your heart. (Is. 40:11.)

"I praise You, Jesus, for helping me to love and forgive myself because God loves and forgives me. Amen."

Psalm 107:20 says: "He (God) sent forth his word and healed them..." (*NIV*). Use God's Word as mental therapy. Apply it constantly to the problem areas of your life, and it *will* heal them!

Prayer: "Lord, I thank You that You are showing me a way to truly change my life so that it will be transformed and I will become more and more like You. I choose to use Your Word every day in my life to bring my whole being into the freedom and confidence that You desire for me as Your child.

"In Jesus' Name, Amen."

Today's Scripture Reading: Psalm 138

Week 5 Day 2
You Are Unique

For you have created my inmost being; you knit me together in my mother's womb.

I praise you because I am fearfully and wonderfully made.

Psalm 139:13,14a NIV

It is wonderful to contemplate how God knew us and planned for us even before we were born. At the moment of your conception He had thousands of choices, yet He chose to form the unique being that is *you*.

It is really amazing that every flower, every leaf, every snowflake, and every person is truly one-of-a-kind. God is the ultimate Creator. Even common sense and logical thinking will tell you that what you are is not a mistake.

Therefore, you can truthfully and confidently affirm: **"I am God's child, uniquely made in His image. I never devalue myself."**

56

When you really begin to know in your inner being that you are unique and special, you will also know that it is not pleasing to God for you to put yourself down or have feelings of inferiority.

Have you ever said things like this about yourself: "I'm so dumb, I just can't learn"; "I'm really stupid"; "I'd forget my head if it weren't attached"; "I'm really a klutz"? If you have, decide now never to make such negative statements again. If you will change your concept of yourself, you will soon become a new person — old negative depressed thoughts will be replaced with new positive ones.

Link today's affirmation with the scripture in Psalm 139, and also with these two verses:

"Therefore, if anyone is in Christ, he is a new creation; the old has gone, the new has come!" (2 Cor. 5:17 *NIV*).

"Don't you know that you yourselves are God's temple and that God's Spirit lives in you?...for God's temple is sacred, and you are that temple" (1 Cor. 3:16,17 *NIV*).

Replacing feelings of inferiority with God's Word is an effective way to rid yourself of those negative feelings and to become the person God had in mind when He created you.

Prayer: "Lord, I thank You for making me just as I am. I repent of the sins of self-pity and self-depreciation. I turn from them and choose to accept Your view of me. I praise You, Father, for giving me the ability and the means to change myself into Your image.

"In Christ's Name, Amen."

Today's Scripture Reading: Psalm 139:1-18,23,24

Week 5 Day 3
Your Blueprint

Show me your ways, O Lord, teach me your paths; guide me in your truth and teach me, for you are God my Savior, and my hope is in you all day long.

Psalm 25:4,5 NIV

In his book, *The Soul's Sincere Desire**, Glenn Clark talks about what our inner person longs to do. Some of the

*Little, Brown & Co., Boston, 1953.

thoughts I'm sharing with you today were "inspired" by what he wrote.

Many times we waste much time and energy trying to be what we are not, looking at other people and wishing we were like them.

We need to make a careful evaluation of our natural abilities and our inner desires in order to accurately discern what kind of things we are to be doing in life.

For instance, I thoroughly enjoy working with children in the 4-to-6-year-old age group. I am the logical choice to be a teacher of a kindergarten department of a Sunday School (which I was for several years — I loved the children and they loved Sunday School and me). Now children that age can get on your nerves if you don't really enjoy working with them. If you honestly don't, then you shouldn't feel it is your "duty" or "call" to do so. You would be doing the wrong thing, both for yourself and the children.

Is there some certain thing you have always wanted to do, such as write, paint pictures or fly an airplane? If so, that is probably something you could and should do.

For years my mother thought she would enjoy painting. She was in her 70s when she started taking lessons. She did not become famous like Grandma Moses, but she did greatly enjoy painting as a pastime and her pictures have brought joy to others.

I would like to encourage you to begin doing something within the next few days you have always thought you would like to do. Don't say, "I can't sew...paint...play the piano" or whatever. Choose something that intrigues you and start doing it. Your life will become much richer and you will be more fulfilled.

Do you "hate" your job? Then perhaps you are in the wrong career field. If at all possible, change jobs. Find one that gives you deep satisfaction, one that you truly enjoy doing.

Perhaps you are a wife and mother and feel "locked into" keeping house and raising children, but don't really enjoy it all that much. I am not suggesting that you take a full-time job outside the home to find fulfillment. But I do suggest that you find a hobby, possibly a part-time job (not over 20 hours a week). Do some volunteer work and/or take some college or correspondence courses. It just might change your whole outlook on life.

I am blessed in that I enjoy housework, cooking, cleaning and doing laundry. I also thoroughly enjoyed raising my children. But I still have diversions such as gardening, writing, refinishing antique furniture and ministering to people.

I consider myself blessed indeed to be one who gets to stay home all day and be "just a housewife." I can't remember the last time I was bored or had nothing to do. So actually, I'm getting to do my "soul's sincere desire." And I praise the Lord He has allowed it!

Prayer: "Father, I come to You in Jesus' Name sincerely desiring to know Your plan for my life. I know that You want me to be happy and fulfilled. In the next few days and weeks as I look objectively at my real self, I ask that You guide me in finding the right thing to be doing so I can grow and blossom in the way You have planned, the way that is best for me and also for those around me.

"In the Name of Jesus, Amen."

Today's Scripture Reading: Psalm 25:1-15,20,21

Week 5 Day 4
You Are Wonderfully Made

Don't you know that you yourselves are God's temple and that God lives in you?...for God's temple is sacred, and you are that temple.

1 Corinthians 3:16,17 NIV

Do you remember how beautiful and perfect God's temple was in the Old Testament? Do you remember the details He gave in His directions on how it should be built? God went to great care to be sure His temple was perfect and beautiful in every way.

Have you then considered how wondrously your body is made? Have you ever thought about its intricate detail? Think of all the many inner parts of your body and how they function together in perfect harmony to keep you alive and healthy. Specialists in the medical field can spend years studying just one organ of the body, such as the heart, and still not know all there is to know about it. And this is just the physical body or "flesh."

Now consider your mind. Think of all the memories, facts, ideas and knowledge stored there! The human mind and its functioning is truly incomprehensible!

How careful we should be to take care of this body and mind of ours! Just as God wanted no contamination in His temple in the Old Testament, I'm sure He desires that we keep our bodies (His temple) free from harmful substances (junk food, cigarettes, alcohol and drugs). To function correctly, our bodies need rest, exercise and proper nutrition.

What about mind contamination? In today's world, it is easy for our minds to become polluted — thanks to the television industry, x-rated movies and the abundance of pornographic literature available. These things should have *no place* in the mind of one who is God's temple! (If this type of thing is a temptation to you, see the devotional on purity — Week 9 Day 4.)

God will give you control over your mind and body as you use His Word in your daily life.

Prayer: "Lord, I recognize that I am 'fearfully and wonderfully made.' I ask forgiveness for the sins I've committed against my body and the things I've done that have contaminated my mind. I repent and turn from these things. I determine in my will to allow You to have control of my body and mind so they will be disciplined in your ways. Thank You that I am Your temple and that You reside in me to help me bring glory to Your Name.

"In Jesus' Name, Amen."

Today's Scripture Reading: 1 Thessalonians 4:1-12

Week 5 Day 5
You Are a New Creation

Therefore, if anyone is in Christ, he is a new creation; the old has gone, the new has come!

2 Corinthians 5:17 NIV

Yesterday we talked about the body and mind. They are important and should be cared for ''as unto the Lord.'' But today let's consider your spirit. You *have* a body and a mind, but you *are* a spirit.

Your spirit is what is made new at the moment of salvation (or being born again). After conversion, you experience changes in your mind and perhaps in your body, but the thing that is immediately made new is your spirit.

God's top priority for you is that your spirit be born again unto Him. Then He wants your mind renewed (Rom. 12:2), and your body disciplined into subjection to your spirit.

In the past, many people, including me, have not understood how to effect this change. Now we have discovered that this disciplining and training is done through and with the Word of God. I have found that the most effective way to bring about desired changes in my body, mind and spirit is by making positive affirmations (linked with correlating scriptures relating to the specific area in which I need growth or correction). This approach brings my mind and body into line with my spirit so that all are harmoniously functioning in the way God planned and desires.

Since God's Word is spirit and life (John 6:63.), it is an effective instrument in nurturing and healing all three areas of our being.

For a long time, our society has realized that in order to function properly our physical bodies must have proper nutrition and care. More recently, we have discovered and emphasized our psychological and emotional needs. I was happy to notice recently in a secular magazine an article, written by a noted psychologist, which stressed our need to give attention and care to the moral and spiritual development of our children.

This development is accomplished through spiritual training; and spiritual training, to be effective, must be based on the Word of God.

Prayer: "Thank You, Father, for giving me a new spirit. I praise You that Your Word can be used to instruct and heal in every area of my life, so that I am made fully able to walk in Your ways and do Your perfect will in my life. "In Jesus' healing Name, Amen."

Today's Scripture Reading: Psalm 51:6-15

Week 5 Day 6
Free In Him

It is for freedom that Christ has set us free. Stand firm, then, and do not let yourselves be burdened again by a yoke of slavery.
Galatians 5:1 NIV

Many people in this world have died for the cause of freedom. Recently, we were reminded of how strong is that drive for freedom, when two families from East Germany risked their lives to escape to West Germany in a home-made hot air balloon.

Political freedom is very important. But even more important is freedom in our inner beings, our spirit and heart. Your "inner healing" has given you this freedom.

If Satan attempts to make you feel as if you are still in bondage, use today's affirmation and suggested scriptures against him, and he will flee from you.

One beautiful thing this freedom does for you is to release you from your past guilts, fears, hurtful memories and resentments. This true freedom is one thing Satan does not want you to experience. Through deceit and false feelings he will attempt to put his "yoke of slavery" back upon you.

God's "way of escape" from this bondage is His Word. Use it against Satan, and you will be victorious and will safeguard your freedom.

Prayer: "Thank You, Father, that I am free, and that I no longer rely on my feelings, which may sometimes revert

to my old ways. I praise You that I now know to rely on Your Word, that I know the truth and the truth sets me free. (John 8:32.) Amen.''

Today's Scripture Reading: John 8:31-41

Affirmation: ''I am forgiven and set free in Christ Jesus.''

Affirmation Scriptures: John 8:36; Galatians 5:1,13; 2 Corinthians 3:17; Hebrews 2:14,15; Psalm 119:32,45.

Week 5 Day 7
Free to Be Real

I run in the path of your commands, for you have set my heart free.

Psalm 119:32 NIV

One other area in which you are now free is your relationship with others. You no longer have to maintain a phony image. You are free to be open with people, to be real.

In the past, you may have felt, ''If other people really knew me, they wouldn't like me.'' Now, you have nothing to hide. You will find that people will be drawn to you because they will sense the wholeness that is in you.

People around you will begin to change. Part of that change will come about because you will begin to see them differently. But it is also true that they will begin to be different because God's Spirit is now free to work through you to change them for the better.

You will also find that as you go along in time, using these affirmations, you will become more and more free.

You will be freer to give and to accept love.

You will be freer to love others without condemning them.

You will feel free to try out new ideas, get a different job, be who you really are. You will no longer feel you have to conform to the crowd for fear of what others might think.

You will be free to be your own unique self, created in God's image.

Prayer: "Lord, I praise You for setting me free and that each day I can grow in that freedom. I thank You that I am pure and whole inside so I no longer have anything to hide from others. Thank You for Your forgiveness that was provided for me through Christ Jesus.

"Amen."

Today's Scripture Reading: Psalm 119:30-48

Week 6
Acquiring Confidence

Week 6 Day 1
Self-Confidence

Being confident of this, that he who began a good work in you will carry it on to completion until the day of Christ Jesus.

Philippians 1:6

A good work has been begun in you. God will continue His good work in you until it is complete — if you continue to be open to Him.

You are able to remain open to God, allowing Him to work in your life, by cultivating His Word within you.

Do you remember the parable of the sower? (Luke 8:5-15.) The seed which was sown represented the Word of God. The good soil which yielded a plentiful harvest represented those people who heard the Word, held fast to it and through perseverance produced fruit.

Through these devotionals, you have now heard the Word. As you hold fast to it (memorize it, meditate upon it and put it into action), you will produce fruit. Fruit that will benefit you in terms of love, joy and peace. Fruit that will involve others — leading them to salvation and healing.

Prayer: "I thank You, Lord, that I can know that You are working in me and that You will not fail to bring good things into my life. I praise You for the peace and joy that are within me. Help me to persevere in walking in Your ways.

"In Jesus' Name, Amen."

Today's Scripture Reading: Luke 8:4-15

Week 6 Day 2
Peace of Mind

Do not be anxious about anything, but in everything, by prayer and petition, with thanksgiving, present your requests to

God. And the peace of God, which transcends all understanding, will guard your hearts and your minds in Christ Jesus.

Philippians 4:6,7 NIV

At one time or another in his life, everyone has experienced anxiety. Many people who are anxious and afraid do not consider fear a sin. Is it? Where does fear come from? The Bible tells us, ''...perfect love drives out fear'' (1 John 7:18 *NIV*). God is perfect love.

Many times in the Bible Jesus admonishes us not to fear, worry or be anxious. Fearful people are not at their best. It is hard for them to do what needs to be done for the Lord because their fear holds them back. Therefore, it seems correct to assume that fear comes from, and is encouraged by, Satan.

In fact, fear is one of the first things that entered this world when man succumbed to Satan's lie. Remember when God came back to the Garden of Eden after man had sinned? Adam and Eve hid themselves from His presence. When God asked, ''Where are you?'', Adam answered, ''...I was afraid...so I hid'' (Gen. 3:9,10 *NIV*).

Fearfulness is certainly not God's best for you. You *can* overcome fear in your life.

Prayer: ''Father, I accept Your peace and confidence in my heart and mind. I release all my fears to Your healing light. Help me as I use Your Word to defeat fear in my life.

''In the Name of Jesus, Amen.''

Today's Scripture Reading: 1 John 4:18

Affirmation: ''I am confident and secure because Jesus is within me.''

Affirmation Scriptures: Psalm 27:1,3,13, 112:7; Isaiah 12:2, 32:17; 1 John 4:18; Romans 8:15; Hebrews 4:16; John 14:27; James 3:18 (AMP).

Week 6 Day 3
Courage

''Be strong and courageous. Do not be afraid...for the Lord your God goes with you; he will never leave you nor forsake you.''

Deuteronomy 31:6 NIV

What wonderful words of encouragement! God is with you. He will never leave you nor forsake you! Sometimes we go through times when it seems that God has left us to face life all alone. It seems that He is far away from us, but He is not. He is still right there with us.

In fact, because of Jesus and the Holy Spirit, God is within us. Jesus said, ''...the kingdom of God is within you'' (Luke 17:21 *NIV*). Perhaps you have been waiting until heaven to see the kingdom of God. You need not wait.

When you realize the truth of God's kingdom being here and now and within you, it opens up many new ideas.

Consider: What is God's kingdom? Power, abundance, perfect health, peace, love, joy and light. Can all this be within you? Yes, if God's kingdom is fully come into you, all these wonderful things exist within you right now!

Prayer: ''I praise You, Lord, that Your kingdom is within me. I thank You that You have 'qualified (me) to share in the inheritance of the saints in the kingdom of light,' and that I have been 'brought...into the kingdom of the Son (You) love' (Col. 1:12,13 *NIV*). May the reality of Your kingdom in me be fully impressed on my spirit and mind.

''In Christ's Name, Amen.''

Today's Scripture Reading: Colossians 1:9-23

Week 6 Day 4
Confidence in the Lord

Let us then approach the throne of grace with confidence, so that we may receive mercy and find grace to help us in our time of need.

Hebrews 4:16 NIV

Who has not had a time of need? Our needs may be spiritual, emotional, physical or financial. Can God help in all of these areas? Certainly.

How do we approach the throne in confidence? We have confidence when we know what God's Word says about our area of need. Confidence is very closely related to faith. Romans 10:17 says, ''...faith cometh by hearing, and hearing by the word of God.''

Therefore, if you feel that your faith (and/or confidence) needs a boost, it can be bolstered and increased through the hearing of the Word of God. Which is the reason I suggest you make your affirmations out loud — so you can *hear* God's Word in your own ears. Not only to renew your mind, but also to let that Word sink down into your spirit, producing faith and confidence.

We have been taught to read God's Word daily, but few of us have used that Word each day of our life to meet the common needs and problems of daily existence.

In the past few years, I have learned to make use of God's Word to meet my everyday needs. For instance: Derin and I are in a faith ministry, which means we do not charge for our counseling or classes. As a result, we have no fixed income. Therefore, our money flow is not consistent. Sometimes the amount coming in has been less than needed to cover our expenses. Instead of allowing Satan to use this situation to discourage me, I consistently confess scriptures about God's financial provision and prosperity.

It works! I praise God that I know it is His will (as revealed in His Word) for His children to have all their needs met fully — plus enough resources left over to be able to give generously to others! (2 Cor. 9:8,11.)

Prayer: "Father, I thank You for Your Word that I may use in my life to bring about confidence — both confidence in myself, and faith and confidence in You. Please help me to remember to use Your Word in every situation to meet my daily needs.

"In Jesus' Name, Amen."

Today's Scripture Reading: 1 John 3:21—4:6

Week 6 Day 5
Perseverance

So do not throw away your confidence; it will be richly rewarded. You need to persevere so that when you have done the will of God, you will receive what he has promised.

Hebrews 10:35,36 NIV

I wonder how many times I have "thrown away my confidence" and, instead of agreeing with the Word of God, have allowed Satan to trick me into making a negative confession — right when the answer was almost manifested!

Perseverance is sometimes very difficult, especially when the answer is long delayed. Notice the three things we are to do to receive our answer: 1) Maintain our confidence, 2) do the will of God, and 3) persevere. When faith and confidence are linked with perseverance, *then* we are richly rewarded and receive what God has promised.

I have found that the best weapon to use against Satan when he comes to discourage me from "holding fast" is simply to quote scripture to him. The devil knows that God's Word is true, so using this "sword of the Spirit" against him is the best and surest way to defeat the enemy.

Prayer: " 'Lord, when doubts fill my mind, when my heart is in turmoil, quiet me and give me renewed hope and cheer' (Ps. 94:19 TLB). I thank You, Father, that my confidence is in You and Your Word, which is established forever. I praise You that Your Word is sinking deep into my spirit to guide me in all my ways.

"In Christ's Name, Amen."

Today's Scripture Reading: Hebrews 10:19-39

Week 6 Day 6
Freedom from Fear

For God hath not given us the spirit of fear; but of power, and of love, and of a sound mind.

2 Timothy 1:7

Reoccurring throughout the Bible are such statements as these: "Fear not"; "Do not be afraid"; "Fret not"; "Be anxious in nothing"; and "Don't worry about tomorrow." How can we really be believing God's Word and still be worrying? If we are living in anxiety, then we are not living what we profess! God does not give us a spirit of fear. That spirit comes from Satan.

What does God give to replace fear? According to today's verse, He gives us a spirit of:

1. *Power*: "...you will receive power when the Holy Spirit comes on you..." (Acts 1:8 *NIV*). "...it is He who is giving you power..." (Deut. 8:18 *NAS*).

2. *Love*: "...perfect love drives out fear" (1 John 4:18 *NIV*). When perfect loves exists between us and another person, there is no fear in that relationship. God's perfect love toward us (and our love toward Him) causes us to be in complete obedience to Him. Such love gives us reassurance, trust and confidence, while driving away all fear.

3. *A sound mind*: "...whatever is true, whatever is noble, whatever is right, whatever is pure, whatever is lovely, whatever is admirable — if anything is excellent or praiseworthy — think about such things" (Phil. 4:8 *NIV*). A sound mind is the result of right thinking. Right thinking, consistently, is possible through being thoroughly grounded in God's Word — which is true, noble, right, pure, lovely, admirable, excellent and praiseworthy!

The way to rid yourself permanently of fear is to *always* use God's Word against it.

Prayer: "Father, I confess that at times I have let fear, anxiety and worry come into my life. I ask Your forgiveness for this wrong. I accept Your help to turn away from old fearful thought patterns. I now commit myself to saying Your Word each day as I replace fear with power, love and a sound mind.

"In Jesus' Name, Amen."

Today's Scripture Reading: Psalm 27

Week 6 Day 7
Security

...a righteous man will be remembered forever.

He will have no fear of bad news; his heart is steadfast, trusting in the Lord.

His heart is secure, he will have no fear.

Psalm 112:6b,7,8 NIV

One basic need of mankind is security. As human beings, we seem to have a built-in desire for self-preservation. Because of this desire, we sometimes go to great lengths in our efforts to insure our protection and well being. Many people hoard up large amounts of food in case of disaster. Others fortify their homes with well-stocked storm or bomb shelters. While others purchase and learn to use firearms. Such measures are evidence that people need to feel physically and mentally secure.

But true security does not come from the outside; it comes from the spirit and heart. These verses from Psalms say that the righteous person is steadfast and secure in *heart*. This is real security. It relieves us of being anxious over physical or world situations. God is able (and willing) to keep us safe and secure no matter what the circumstances may be around us.

We have no need to cling to things. (Have you ever seen a hearse pulling a U-Haul trailer?) Our physical body and our possessions will one day drop away, but our spirit is eternally secure in God's kingdom. And Jesus told us, "...the kingdom of God is within you" (Luke 17:21 *NIV*). God's kingdom is not way off up in heaven in the "sweet by and by," but rather it is in *you and me* right now!

You can know the peace, joy and love of that kingdom today, for God's Spirit bears witness with our spirit that we are the children of God. (Rom. 8:16.)

When I was a child, I attended a little one-room country school in Nebraska. It was about a half-mile south of our house so I usually walked to school. I can remember one afternoon when a raging blizzard swept down on the countryside. That day my father met me as soon as school was out. The wind was blowing blinding snow right out of the north, but my father walked ahead of me, blocking the icy gale and leading me to safety and warmth. I had absolutely no fear that we would not get home safe and sound. I was secure in my father's love and care. How much more should we feel secure in our Heavenly Father's faithful, loving hands?

71

Prayer: "Father, I praise You for the noble and good earthly father and grandfather You gave me. They were an example of Your steadfastness and love to me. Help me to feel as secure in Your faithfulness as I did in theirs. Amen."*

Today's Scripture Reading: Psalm 23; Galatians 3:26—4:7

*If you did not have a good earthly father, ask God to heal all the hurts and insecurities caused within you because of that situation and to place within you a correct understanding of His love and care as your Heavenly Father.

Week 7
Establishing Righteousness

Week 7 Day 1
Establishing Righteousness: Spiritually I

And the kingdom and the dominion and the greatness of the kingdom under the whole heavens shall be given to the people of the saints of the most High; His kingdom is an everlasting kingdom, and all the dominions shall serve and obey Him.

Daniel 7:27 AMP

What a powerful verse! We, the saints of the Most High, are given the kingdom and the dominion under the heavens. Couple this verse with Revelation 5:10: ''You have made them to be a kingdom and priests to serve our God, and they will reign on the earth'' (*NIV*).

If we Christians would comprehend and understand and believe these two verses, without wavering, then we would change the whole world in a very short time.

For too long Satan has deceived us into thinking everything that happens here on earth is God's responsibility. He has even managed to convince many Christians that their sickness, poverty and troubles come from God — the ''suffering-for-Jesus'' syndrome! If you have fallen for this lie, here is something new for you to contemplate.

When Adam and Eve were created, the Word of God says: ''And God blessed them; and God said to them, '...rule...over every living thing that moves on the earth' '' (Gen. 1:28 NAS). So man was created to reign on this earth. But through sin, Adam and Eve lost their dominion, and Satan became the god of this world.

In His death and resurrection, Jesus, the Son of God, redeemed the earth and gave dominion over it back to His followers: ''(Christ) disarmed the powers and authorities...triumphing over them by the cross'' (Col. 2:15 *NIV*).

73

As Christians, we need to know how to take our rightful authority and be in charge here on earth. For too long the ungodly have kept the bulk of power (political, financial and even spiritual) under their evil control.

This subversion could not have happened had we Christians understood our authority and power as sons of God. Through the perfect sacrifice of Jesus, God paid the price for His kingdom to come, His will to be done on earth as it is in heaven. Establishing that kingdom and will on this planet is up to you and me!

This is an awesome responsibility! It cannot be fulfilled through a few short prayer sessions. But, I believe, it *can* be done. This week's devotionals should help you discover how.

Prayer: "God of creation, please help me to understand Your Word concerning my authority and dominion here on earth. I desire to walk as Jesus did, in absolute control of every situation in life, with Satan having no hold on me.

"May I learn to walk in this dominion as a king and a priest before You, bringing Your kingdom in my life and in the lives of others.

"In the authority of Jesus' Name, Amen."

Today's Scripture Reading: Mark 4:35—6:7

Week 7 Day 2
Establishing Righteousness: Spiritually II

"...Any kingdom divided against itself is laid waste; and any city or house divided against itself shall not stand."

Matthew 12:25 NAS

The Apostle James speaks of a double-minded man being unstable in all his ways and unable to receive anything from God. (James 1:5-8.) My purpose in these devotionals is to help you to become congruent (unified) in spirit, heart, mind and body.

There are steps one takes to achieve this wholeness: 1) Being born again, 2) receiving the Holy Spirit, 3) having inner healing, 4) renewing the mind, 5) knowing one's identity in Christ, and now, 6) establishing righteousness.

As a non-Christian, or even as a Christian, in your past there have been areas of your life that were controlled by Satan, either because of willful sin, ignorance or perhaps lack of self-control. Many people are unwilling to admit that rather than just weaknesses, besetting sins, carnal tendencies, mistakes or whatever else we may have called them in the past, these things are really strongholds of Satan. At any rate, more than likely, there are still areas of your life in which you know (and Satan knows too!) that you are less than completely victorious! These strongholds of the enemy need to be subdued, cast out and replaced with the wholeness and holiness of God.

Today's prayer, confession and scriptures can do just that. You may not see an instant change, but as you confess correctly, righteousness *will be* established because you are confessing the powerful Word of God which defeats Satan. God Himself watches over His Word to perform it. (Jer. 1:12.)

Prayer: ''Father God, Lord of all, I come against any and all strongholds of Satan in my life. I cast down _____ (name your besetting sin or sins) and say that the devil and all his demons are defeated in this/these area(s).

''I replace this/these stronghold(s) with forgiveness, peace, joy, purity, confidence, and patience. I ask You, Lord, to establish righteousness and Your control in all areas of my spirit, heart, mind and body. Through the power of the Holy Spirit, I choose to be victorious over all the temptations of Satan.

''In the strong Name of Jesus, Amen.''

Today's Scripture Reading: 2 Corinthians 10:3-5

Affirmation: ''In Jesus' Name I cast down any evil influence of Satan in my life. I nullify all negative thoughts and words from the past. From this day forth I establish God's control and His righteousness in my life.''

Affirmation Scriptures: Psalm 103:19 and Luke 17:21 (AMP) (use these two together); Colossians 2:9,10,15; 2 Corinthians 10:4,5; Luke 10:19; Revelation 5:10, 12:11; Psalm 8:6, 115:16; James 4:7.

Week 7 Day 3
Establishing Righteousness: Mentally I

...We demolish arguments and every pretension that sets itself up against the knowledge of God, and we take captive every thought to make it obedient to Christ.

2 Corinthians 10:4b,5 NIV

The knowledge of God comes from knowing His Word. Many Christians have thoughts in their mind that are against the knowledge of God, but they don't even know it because they are so ignorant of what His Word says.

In Hosea 4:6 God tells us, "My people are destroyed for lack of knowledge..." (*AMP*).

Ministers are always preaching that we need more faith, but how many sermons have you heard instructing you on how to have more *knowledge*?

I believe the root of the problem with the Church today is not a lack of faith, but a lack of knowledge on the part of Christians. How can a person have faith for healing, finances, peace or a happy home if he does not know God's Word, His will and His ways in these areas?

Some people have many verses memorized and stored away in their mind, but they haven't prayed and received the revelation — the wisdom or meaning or application — of these verses. Such verses represent only head knowledge, not heart or spirit knowledge.

Once you have the Word of God established in your spirit and heart, then it rises to your defense to defeat the thoughts that come from Satan, demolishing his arguments and pretensions and making your thoughts obedient to Christ.

The Word of God is the way of escape the Lord has provided so you will not fall into temptation. (1 Cor. 10:13.)

Here is a diagram to illustrate this point:

GOD AND HIS TRUTH   ⟶   Positive Results
    YOUR THOUGHT LIFE — THOUGHTS — ATTITUDES — ACTIONS — HABITS
SATAN AND HIS LIES   ⟶   Negative Results

When a thought comes to your mind, you are the one who chooses whether you continue to think negative (Satan-induced) or positive (God-inspired) thoughts. Your thoughts are just the beginning of the process, and what you do with them eventually determines the kind of life you will live.

Prayer: "Dear Father in heaven, I desire true knowledge based on Your Word. I ask You to take the Word I have read and memorized and make it alive in my heart. Help me to destroy quickly every thought from Satan and to meditate on Your words day and night. May only truth be kept in my mind. May wisdom always be my goal.

"In the Name of Jesus, Who is made unto me wisdom, Amen."

Today's Scripture Reading: Philippians 4:1-9

Week 7 Day 4
Establishing Righteousness: Mentally II

Let this same attitude and purpose and [humble] mind be in you which was in Christ Jesus.

Philippians 2:5 AMP

To have the attitude and purpose, the mind of Christ — is this possible? It must be or we wouldn't be instructed to have it!

Christ knew the will of His Father, God. He knew what God had said in the Old Testament. He was directed by the Holy Spirit. He completely submitted His will to the will of His Father.

For us to have the mind of Christ, we must do the same! We must know the will of God by knowing His Word, be led and directed by the Holy Spirit, and be in submission to the will of God.

In Romans 12:2, we are instructed to be transformed by the renewing of our mind, *then* we will know the good, pleasing and perfect will of God.

There are so many Christians who say, "I just don't know God's will for me. I don't know what He wants me to do." When you hear someone make that statement, start checking his Word level. See if he has his mind renewed in God's Word. If not, that is what he needs to be doing, instead of going from Christian friend to Christian friend taking an opinion poll!

As humans we always want to know everything in advance. God's whole will is not always revealed to us all at once. Often it is a step-by-step revelation. For instance: When Derin and I started this ministry, we knew it was God's will that we have a ministry of teaching and healing. So we began a weekly meeting to do just that. Later, we knew we were to have meetings in various churches, so we did that as God directed. After about four years, God told Derin to go on television. Now we have a program on TV and a daily radio program.

When we began our ministry five years ago, we didn't know all this would come about. God has led us step by step, gradually revealing His will to us as we have followed Him in trust and obedience.

Prayer: "Dear Lord, please help me to have the mind of Christ. Establish a forgiving, loving, peaceful spirit within me. Reveal Your will to me as I renew my mind in Your Word. Then give me the ability and determination to walk in it.

"In Jesus' Name, Amen."

Today's Scripture Reading: 1 Corinthians 2 (The Amplified Bible, if possible)

Week 7 Day 5
Establishing Righteousness: Physically

Since we have these promises, dear friends, let us purify ourselves from everything that contaminates body and spirit, perfecting holiness out of reverence for God.

2 Corinthians 7:1 NIV

Derin and I receive many letters from Christians who are still fighting the battle to overcome habits such as overeating, smoking, drinking to excess and taking drugs. For many, the root of these habits is in their spirit and mind.

As your spirit is healed and your mind renewed, you will be freed of these types of bad habits.

(Later in this devotional there is a whole week devoted to overcoming these individual habits that you do not want controlling you. If you are "desperate" to be free in this area, feel free to go to Week 9 and begin confessing victory over the habits you need to conquer.)

Determine to be steadfast and diligent in this area. For a long time now I have confessed God's control over my eating habits. I am still not satisfied with my self-control in eating, but I am determined to have victory in this area of my life, so daily I continue to confess God's control and several scriptures.

I liken some habits to the bind weed in my garden — pull them out and they come back, pull them out and they come back, over and over. Other weeds, such as fire weed, once pulled out by the roots, are gone. I prefer fire weeds, but I don't give up on the bind weed. I keep on hoeing and pulling to get rid of it. I am determined to have a weed-free garden. I am just as determined to have a controlled, disciplined body.

Prayer: "Dear Father God, I ask that You show me why I continue to have this habit I don't want. If there are root causes in my spirit or heart, reveal them to me so I can yield them up to You for healing. Change the attitudes in my mind that need to be changed, so I can overcome this habit. Cleanse and purify my body from the ill effects of _____ (overeating, smoking, drinking, drugs, etc.).

"Take away my desire for _____ **and establish temperance and self-control in my body. Help me to see my body as the temple of Your Holy Spirit and to live accordingly.**

"In Jesus' strong Name, Amen."

Today's Scripture Reading: 1 Corinthians 9:24-27

Affirmation: "As an act of my will, I place my spirit, mind and body in God's control. I am victorious over wrong attitudes and harmful habits. The Holy Spirit rules my whole being."

Affirmation Scriptures: Romans 8:5,6; 1 Corinthians 3:16, 6:19,20; Galatians 5:16,25; John 6:63; Philippians 3:21; Romans 8:1 (AMP); 1 Thessalonians 5:23 (AMP); 1 Peter 4:1,2 (AMP).

Week 7 Day 6
Living as a Child of Light

For you were once in darkness, but now you are light in the Lord. Live as children of light (for the fruit of the light consists in all goodness, righteousness and truth) and find out what pleases the Lord.

Ephesians 5:8-10 NIV

When we live as children of light, we will attract people to Jesus. In Colossians 1:13 Paul tells us that God has rescued us from the dominion of darkness and has brought us into the kingdom of the Son.

There is a great spiritual thirst in the hearts of people today. They need to see the light in God's children to give them hope. When you are living a holy life in spirit, mind and body, you will find that people are drawn to you. Leading them to the Lord will then become easy.

This translation of Matthew 13:43 by Kenneth Wuest is taken literally from the Greek: "Then those who are righteous, like the sun when it bursts through the clouds which have hidden it, shall shine forth through the world of evil, dissipating the darkness of sin which has obscured the good and veiled the true glory of their righteousness, in the kingdom of their Father."*

As righteous ones, our light is to be shining before men bringing glory to God. (Matt. 5:16.) And it will, as we walk in right ways in all areas of our life.

*The New Testament: An Expanded Translation by Kenneth S. Wuest. Copyright © 1961 by Wm. B. Erdman Publishing Co., Grand Rapids, Michigan.

In my own life, for over a year now I have been striving to establish righteousness in spirit, mind and body and to understand and use my dominion. I'm not satisfied yet with my accomplishments, but I will not give up!

I believe the true desires of my heart are perfect before God. As I discipline my mind and body in the Word, I believe they will line up more and more with my heart (or spirit).

The book that first inspired me to begin this spiritual journey was *I Will Lift Up Mine Eyes** by Glenn Clark. His writings changed my life because they challenged me to walk on a much higher plane in my relationship to God than I had ever attempted before.

My prayer is that as you read this devotional, you too will be inspired and challenged to live in such a way that you become a reflector of the Lord's glory, being "transformed into His likeness with ever-increasing glory" (2 Cor. 3:18 *NIV*).

Prayer: "Lord of Light, I bow in Your presence and pray that Your light will permeate my whole being — spirit, heart, mind and body. I command all darkness to leave, and I receive Your pure and holy light into every area of my life. I choose to walk in Your light each day.

"In the Name of Jesus, the Son of Light, Amen."

Today's Scripture Reading: 2 Corinthians 3:12—4:18

Week 7 Day 7
Being Complete

...how much more will those who receive God's abundant provision of grace and of the gift of righteousness reign in life through the one man, Jesus Christ.

Romans 5:17 NIV

For in Him all the fulness of Diety dwells in bodily form,

*Harper & Row, Publisher, New York and Evanston, copyright 1937.

and in Him you have been made complete, and He is the head over all rule and authority.

Colossians 2:9,10 NAS

''...you have been made complete...'' to ''...reign in life through Jesus Christ.''

The Word of God says it, so we dare to believe it. Since the Bible is God's revealed will, His desire for us must be completeness in spirit, mind and body, and a lifestyle of ruling and reigning here on earth.

Therefore, that should be our goal. We start by taking authority over our own mind and body. The next step is to take dominion over own own family and possessions. Then, we branch out to exercise rule over other areas, such as the weather.

(For deeper insight into how this can be done correctly and effectively, I recommend reading Agnes Sanford's book, *Creation Waits*.*)

This weeks's devotions have been teaching you how to rule your own self in God's righteous ways. In the week on family relationships, I will be teaching on how a family is ordered in God's ways and established in righteousness.

Apparently this was done by my grandparents and parents because as far as I know all my aunts, uncles and first cousins are Christians. And I know positively that my sister, brothers, and all their children are believers. What a wonderful heritage!

Prayer: ''Lord, I desire to have righteousness established in every area of my life — in my spirit, my mind, my body and in my family. I ask for wisdom to do this according to Your will and Your ways. May wholeness and holiness be always my goal.

''In the perfect Name of Jesus, Amen.''

Today's Scripture Reading: Colossians 3:17; Ephesians 5:1-18 (If possible, read these in *The Amplified Bible*)

*Logos International, Plainfield, N.J., copyright (not dated).

Week 8
Increasing Your Word Power

Week 8 Day 1
Control of the Tongue: What Do You Say?

If anyone is never at fault in what he says, he is a perfect man, able to keep his whole body in check....

...but no man can tame the tongue.

James 3:2b, 8a NIV

All the words of my mouth are righteous — upright and in right standing with God; there is nothing contrary to truth or crooked in them.

Proverbs 8:8 AMP

At first reading, these two verses may seem to contradict each other, but they do not. Just because man cannot tame his tongue does not mean that it is not controllable; it just means that man can not do it alone. God must have control of man's tongue, then he can be made capable of being ''never at fault in what he says.''

This week we will be reading many verses which emphasize the power of words and the importance of what we say. This is a key concept of the Bible. Through it we learn one of the ways of God.

How can your words be controlled by God? By knowing what His Word says in every area and then by saying only what agrees with His Word. *Your* words need to agree with *God's* words.

How many times have you said phrases such as these: ''That makes me sick''; ''You drive me crazy''; ''That blows my mind''; ''I was tickled to death''; or, ''I'm scared to death this or that will happen''? Do such statements agree with God's words? Certainly not! God says: ''...my words....are health to a man's whole body'' (Prov. 4:20,22 NIV). Paul tells us: ''For God hath not given us the spirit of fear, but...of a sound mind'' (2 Tim. 1:7). And our Lord

Jesus said: ''I have come that they might have life, and have it to the full'' (John 10:10 *NIV*).

When you say negative things about yourself and others, you do not plant the good seeds of God's Word which can produce a good harvest in your life and theirs. Today's prayer will pull out the ''weeds'' of wrong speaking. Then you can start affirming and planting good seeds based on the Word of God.

Prayer: ''Father, I come to You in Jesus' Name. I confess and repent of the sin of wrong words in my life. I now receive Your forgiveness for them. And now, by the blood of the Lamb and the word of my testimony, I nullify, reject and cancel every word that I have ever spoken in my whole life that was not in agreement with Your Word, every word upon which Jesus and Your holy angels could not act.

''Lord, I receive this forgiveness in my heart, mind and body. I resolve from this time forward to let You keep watch over my words, guarding everything I say. 'Set a guard over my mouth, O Lord; keep watch over the door of my lips' (Ps. 141:3 *NIV*).

''In Jesus' Name, Amen.''

Today's Scripture Reading: James 3

Affirmation: ''I have given the Holy Spirit control of my tongue. He guards everything I say.''

Affirmation Scriptures: (Choose at least three verses from this week's devotionals and say them in conjunction with this affirmation.)

Week 8 Day 2
Speak Life

The tongue has the power of life and death.
Proverbs 18:21a NIV

The writer of Proverbs was King Solomon. Surely he understood power because he had a great deal of it, including the power of life and death over those he ruled. Fortunately for Solomon's subjects, he also possessed a great deal of wisdom.

We also need wisdom — especially in this area of speaking. I suggest you take time this week to read the whole book of Proverbs, especially noting all it has to say about the tongue, mouth, lips and speech. By so doing, you can add to your understanding of God's ways.

It should be sobering to us to realize that the power of life and death resides in that small, hard-to-control member of our body, the tongue. How important it is then that we allow God to be in control of our tongues and that we be careful that what we say is in alignment with the Word!

I know that the talk around our house has changed since my husband and I have come to realize the importance of what we say. Derin and I keep a constant "check" on each other's speech. When one of us makes a negative statement, the other one will ask, "Is that really what you meant to say?" We are helping each other guard our speech. We want our tongues to always promote life and never death!

Prayer: "Father, help me to realize the importance of what I say. I want the words I say to bring about life and good things in my home. I pray with the Psalmist, 'Let the words of my mouth and the meditation of my heart, be acceptable in thy sight, O Lord, my strength, and my redeemer' (Ps. 19:14).

"In Christ's Name, Amen."

Today's Scripture Reading: Proverbs 10:11-32

Week 8 Day 3
Speak Love

Do not let any unwholesome talk come out of your mouths, but only what is helpful for building up.

Ephesians 4:29 NIV

When Satan is unable to trip up a Christian by getting him to lie, steal or commit adultery, he loves to resort to the "less noticeable" sins of gossip, strife and slander. How quickly many of us fall into his trap of unwholesome talk!

When unsaved people see such behavior in us, they use it as an excuse for not becoming a Christian. As disciples of Christ, we are to be recognized by the world because of our love for one another. But when we are backbiting and gossiping about each other, outsiders certainly don't see love being manifested!

I'm not complaining about the persecution to which Derin and I (and our own personal ministry) have been subjected, because it has caused me to grow spiritually. But it has saddened me to realize that many of the unkind and even untrue things that have been said about us and our ministry have come from church people. Their Christian love has not been evident.

One of my friends was kind enough to call and ask if something she had been told about us was true. At least she had the courage to find out the truth before she passed the story on to others. How many times have we repeated gossip without even bothering to check to see for ourselves whether it was actually true or not?

When a loved one in our family makes a mistake or sins, how careful we are to keep it quiet! Do we use the same care when one of our Christian brothers falls into sin? Is our talk ''only what is helpful for building others up'' and motivated from a heart of love?

Prayer: ''Father, forgive me for the sin of gossip in my life. I repent of the unloving and unkind words I have said to or about other people. From now on may I speak only in love and compassion.

''In Jesus' Name, Amen.''

Today's Scripture Reading: Ephesians 4

Week 8 Day 4
Speak Grace

Let your conversation be always full of grace, seasoned with salt, so that you may know how to answer everyone.

Colossians 4:6 NIV

Have you ever said something which later you wished you could erase? Probably everyone has. As you thought

86

back on your remarks, you began to worry that what you had said might be repeated. You wondered how you would defend yourself or answer the person about whom you had spoken ill. That is an uncomfortable situation to be in!

This verse, when its advice is followed in your daily conversation, will eliminate that problem. Since grace has to do with forgiveness, love and favor, if your conversation is full of it, you will never say anything unkind, anything you will later regret.

This verse also indicates that you will have wisdom in what you say, knowing how to answer the questions of people who do not understand God's ways.

Knowing how to answer also indicates that you were really listening while the other person was talking. Listen with your spirit and heart — not just with your mind — then you can answer people wisely.

We are to be the salt of the earth. Our conversation should show this as we give correct counsel and advice to others. A conversation "seasoned with salt" is not bland and boring, but gives people answers and hope for a solution to their problems.

Prayer: "Dear Lord, may what I say be so governed by Your Spirit that it benefits not only me, but others around me. I ask that my words be a blessing to all and a curse to no one. I say that my words will be 'full of grace,' building others up, because I speak with wisdom.

"In Jesus' Name, Amen."

Today's Scripture Reading: Proverbs 12:5-22

Week 8 Day 5
Speak With Care

"For out of the overflow of the heart the mouth speaks. A good man brings good things out of the good stored up in him, and the evil man brings evil things out of the evil stored up in him. But I tell you that men will have to give account on the day of judgment for every careless word they have spoken."

Matthew 12:34b-36 NIV

Here Jesus used some strong language in dealing with the Pharisees. He taught that what a person says, good or evil, actually comes from his heart.

What the Pharisees were saying against Christ was actually coming from the evil that was stored up in them. It is interesting to note that they considered themselves to be the religious leaders of their day; they felt self-righteous because of their strict obedience to the laws. Jesus saw past their "respectability" and into the corruption of their inner being.

There are Christians today who look very "good" on the outside. They dress correctly, they attend church faithfully and they are busy in the work of the church. But when they talk, their words are (at best) careless and (at worst) malicious gossip. As fellow Christians, we tend to overlook their "indiscretions," but this verse says that God doesn't. One day He will call them to account for their words.

The non-Christians don't overlook such behavior either. They call it hypocrisy, and it causes them not only to question the sincerity of all Christians but also to doubt the Christian faith.

Jesus' words were powerful and commanded attention and respect. As always, we need to take heed of them and be careful to follow His example.

Prayer: "Father, I repent of careless or idle words in my life. I ask that You make me aware of my words; may they always be controlled by Your Holy Spirit.

"In Jesus' Name, Amen."

Today's Scripture Reading: Matthew 12:22-37

Week 8 Day 6
Speak Good Things

From the fruit of his lips a man is filled with good things as surely as the work of his hands rewards him.

Proverbs 12:14 NIV

As Americans, brought up by and instilled with the "work ethic," we find it difficult to conceive that the words of our mouth can bring us prosperity as surely as "good hard work."

Many people have put their confidence in their own ability to work long, difficult hours and thus earn a living. They look to their own strength, wisdom and capabilities for their security. Such people need to transfer this trust to God who is their true source.

This can be done through the "fruit of the lips," by saying that it is God who blesses and prospers us. If we will think it through, we will realize that God certainly is our true source. For without the physical and mental health He provides, we certainly couldn't sustain ourselves by "hard work" alone.

The economic uncertainty of our world should make all of us, especially us Christians, aware that man's financial systems are not at all dependable.

You will spare yourself much anxiety and frustration if you will truly put your trust in God's financial ways as shown in His Word. (There will be a week's devotionals on finances later in this book.) When you place your confidence in God, you have no need to worry about financial security (as today's scripture reading plainly points out).

Prayer: "Father, I come to You in the Name of Jesus, Your Son. I yield up my concerns over money to You. I confess with my lips that You are my source and that You meet all my needs each day. Amen."

Today's Scripture Reading: Matthew 6:19-34

Week 8 Day 7
Guard Your Tongue

If anyone considers himself religious and yet does not keep a tight rein on his tongue, he deceives himself and his religion is worthless.

James 1:26 NIV

Do you consider yourself a "good Christian" and yet do not have your tongue under control? Then you are deceiving yourself. But the sad thing is that you are *not* deceiving the people around you. You may fool yourself, but others (especially family members) see through such phoniness and hypocrisy because your words are not pure and right, not used only for "building others up."

Such a double standard renders your religion worthless. If you have an uncontrolled tongue, then your witness for Christ among those who need Him so badly has no value. In fact, when talking to people about becoming Christians, I have found that one of the biggest obstacles to their acceptance of the faith is often some "Christian" who has an uncontrolled tongue! I don't like to admit it, but usually this "Christian" is a woman, one who is busy in church work but who also has a "busy tongue" that is quick to condemn, run down, or pass along gossip about other people.

As James has noted, the tongue is very difficult to tame. If we are going to claim that Jesus is Lord in our lives, we must yield this small member of our body to Him and work with the Holy Spirit, using God's Word to control the words we speak.

The results of wrong speaking are often disastrous! But the rewards of right speaking are tremendous!

Prayer: "Dear Lord, may my lips, mouth and tongue be cleansed and blessed by Your Holy Spirit. I ask that He control my words. May everything I say glorify You and Your Son, in whose Name I pray, Amen."

Today's Scripture Reading: Isaiah 6:1-10

90

Week 9
Achieving Self-Control

Week 9 Day 1
Self-Control

Whatever happens, conduct yourselves in a manner worthy of the gospel of Christ.

Philippians 1:27 NIV

There are many stress-producing situations in life. Things that, for the "average person," cause anger, hurt feelings, self-pity or resentment. In the next few days we will be concentrating our attention on control in these areas. This control will be *self*-control (as spoken of in Titus 2:11,12): "For the grace of God that brings salvation has appeared to all men. It teaches us to say 'No' to ungodliness and worldly passions, and to live self-controlled, upright and godly lives in this present age..."

In Galatians 5:22 (*NIV*) the Bible also speaks of self-control as a fruit of the Spirit of God. Christians often talk of being controlled by God. Actually control in our lives needs to be a cooperative effort. We give control to God's Spirit and also learn self-control by disciplining and training our mind and emotions in God's Word.

To do this, it is necessary to know what the Word has to say about the emotions and how we should react as children of God. Self-control is needed in both general and specific areas.

Perhaps you have the feeling you are "out of control" in your life and need help in every area. Here is a prayer you can use:

Prayer: "Father, I yield up control of my life to You and Your Holy Spirit. I ask Your guidance as I use Your Word to discipline and control my emotions and actions.

"In Jesus' Name I pray, Amen."

Today's Scripture Reading: 2 Peter 1:3-11

Week 9 Day 2
Control Over Anger I

...Everyone should be quick to listen, slow to speak and slow to become angry, for man's anger does not bring about the righteous life that God desires.

James 1:19b,20 NIV

Anger may be the most often encountered of all negative emotions. It is also the most defended by Christians. Some deny they are *ever* angry. Others bury their anger deep inside where it produces physical problems like nervousness and irritability, chronic indigestion, ulcers, asthma, migraine headaches — even heart disease. Still others simply excuse their anger by re-defining it as "righteous indignation." (I've encountered very little authentic righteous indignation in my fellow Christians, but I have seen plenty of plain old sinful, selfish anger!)

Rather than deny our anger, we need to recognize it for what it is — sin. We need to ask God's forgiveness for that wrong emotion. This is hard for some Christians to do because they have been brought up with the teaching that once a person is "sanctified" or "Spirit-filled," it is impossible for him to sin. If you are of this persuasion, please ask God to open your eyes to the truth of this matter. (Read carefully 1 John 1:8—2:6.)

I did not gain peace and control in my life until I admitted that my anger was a sin and asked forgiveness for it. Then I did as Tim LaHaye suggests in his book, *Spirit-Controlled Temperaments*.* Each time I became angry, I not only asked God to forgive me, I also prayed that He would help me to break the habit of anger in my life. This was before I knew about inner healing and affirmations, but even then my prayers worked. My incidents of anger dropped dramatically.

It was a pleasant surprise to me and my family to have that old habit of anger almost completely eliminated.

*Tyndale House Publishers, Wheaton, Illinois, copyright 1966.

I suggest that you, too, admit your anger and confess it as sin. Then ask God's forgiveness and use this prayer and affirmation to overcome your anger once and for all.

Prayer: "Father, I confess that I have had the sin of anger in my life. I repent of an unforgiving attitude and bitterness and I turn from them. I ask that You bless me with a peaceful and patient spirit so I may reflect Christ to all I meet.

"In Jesus' Name, Amen."

Today's Scripture Reading: Colossians 3:8-17

Affirmation: "My emotions are controlled by the Holy Spirit. I am patient and kind."

Affirmation Scriptures: Proverbs 14:29, 29:11,22; Ecclesiastes 7:9; Ephesians 4:26,27; 1 Thessalonians 5:14 (AMP); James 1:19,20 (AMP); Colossians 3:12.

Week 9 Day 3
Control Over Anger II

"In your anger do not sin": Do not let the sun go down while you are still angry, and do not give the devil a foothold.
Ephesians 4:26,27 NIV

The first part of verse 26 is a quote from Psalm 4. I believe it indicates that one can be angry, but still not be sinful in his attitude. The key to this control is not to continue in anger, not to carry it on to unforgiveness and bitterness.

Anger is usually not pre-meditated. It rises up in us almost instantaneously before we have time to think about it.

Most people can control the actions prompted by anger. They have learned not to let themselves knock other people around. Fewer people, but still many, have learned not to shout angry words at others. But the hardest part of anger to control is the feeling it produces inside.

To conquer angry feelings, you need to let forgiveness flow through you to whoever has angered you by saying out loud: "Lord, as an act of my will, I allow forgivenesss to flow from You through me to _____. I release and forgive him/her right now."

Then make your affirmation and repeat the related scriptures. If there is one certain person whom you find it particularly difficult to forgive, you may wish to add this sentence to the affirmation: "I have a loving attitude toward _____."

Feelings can and do change through consistent right confession based on God's Word. Your real self is spirit and your new spirit is to control your mind (emotions and attitudes) by use of God's Word.

This passage from Ephesians tells us not to let the sun go down while we are still angry. There is a reason for this counsel. Prolonged anger leads to resentment, bitterness and hatred. These emotions are "killers" because they damage our spirit, mind and body, and our fellowship with God and other people. They "give the devil a foothold" from which he will attempt to destroy us. But, praise the Lord, we can avoid all these negative effects through the power of God's Word!

Prayer: "Father, in Jesus' Name, I release my anger and I forgive those who have caused it. Please take control of my emotions and make me Christ-like in all I say and do.
"In His Name, Amen."

Today's Scripture Reading: Ephesians 4:17—5:21

Week 9 Day 4
Cleansing of Impurity

Create in me a pure heart, O God, and renew a steadfast spirit within me.

Psalm 51:10 NIV

In today's society, the "new morality" (which really should be called the old *im*morality, because it has been with us since the fall of man in the Garden of Eden), has caused many people to feel defiled or "dirty" because of sexual sins.

Some entered into "sex play" as children. Some fell for the lie that "everyone is doing it," and slept with various partners in high school and college. Others had sexual union only with the person they later married, but still feel guilty about their pre-marital relations. Still others have been unfaithful in their marriage.

Some people were sexually abused as children (especially in the case of incest), and others have been raped. All these people must forgive and release the other persons involved. All need to know God's forgiveness and the cleansing of Jesus' blood. Many need to forgive themselves.

All these sexual sins, and any others not mentioned, can be forgiven, cleansed and erased by correct praying and confession of the Word.

Prayer: "Dear Lord, I come before You in humility and repentance. I repent of any and all sexual sin in my life. I ask Your forgiveness. I ask that the energy of Jesus' blood flow from the top of my head to the soles of my feet cleansing me, inside and out, and washing away *all* defilement.

"Lord, make me wholly pure in spirit, mind and body. As an act of my will, I forgive anyone who has defiled me. I also forgive and release myself from sexual sins and I accept Your forgiveness. I am now pure in Your eyes. Thank You, Father, for forgiving and cleansing me.

"In the pure Name of Jesus, Amen."

Today's Scripture Reading: 1 Thessalonians 4:1-12

Affirmation: "I am forgiven and cleansed through the blood of Jesus. I have the purity of Christ in me."

Affirmation Scriptures (Look up, memorize and use at least three of these with your affirmation): *Psalm 51:10, 73:1, 119:9; Matthew 5:8; Acts 15:9; John 1:9; 2 Corinthians 7:1; Philippians 1:9,10; Titus 2:11,12,14; 1 Thessalonians 4:4,7,8 (AMP).*

Week 9 Day 5
Overcoming Lust

For the grace of God that brings salvation has appeared to all men. It teaches us to say "No" to ungodliness and worldly passions, and to live self-controlled, upright and godly lives in this present age.

Titus 2:11,12 NIV

"In this present age" many people's lives are in chaos because they have adopted society's standards in the area of sexual behavior.

Others, who are sincerely trying to live a Christian life, find themselves overwhelmed by the temptations presented to them in magazines, television programs, movies and the sexual appeals in advertising.

I believe that deep down inside everyone knows that sex outside of marriage is wrong. But some people are trying to fool themselves by saying it is all right "as long as it doesn't hurt someone else."

Others would admit that they know illicit sex is wrong, but they seem powerless to control their lust.

I assume that since you are using this devotional, you are a Christian. I also assume that as a Christian you are interested in discovering a better way to deal with temptation and lust. There is a better way. That way is to find out what God says about these subjects and then follow His directives.

The law God gave the children of Israel through Moses declared: "You shall not commit adultery" (Ex. 20:14 *NIV*).

Jesus taught the people of His day: "You have heard that it was said, 'Do not commit adultery.' But I tell you that anyone who looks at a woman lustfully has already committed adultery with her in his heart" (Matt. 5:27,28 *NIV*).

The commandments given to Moses were directed to fleshly men. Jesus gave instructions for our hearts.

So this battle is to be won in the spiritual realm first, then we will be conquerors in the physical realm. How this is done will be presented in the next two devotionals.

Prayer: "Father, I ask Your forgiveness for any time I have not honored You with my body. I ask for forgiveness and release from lust and all sexual impurity. I repent and turn

away from any sexual sin in my life. I determine, through the power of Your Holy Spirit, to walk in purity.

"In the strong Name of Jesus, Amen."

Today's Scripture Reading: 1 Corinthians 6:9-19

Week 9 Day 6
Establishing Purity I

How can a young man keep his way pure? By living according to your word.

Psalm 119:9 NIV

No temptation has seized you except what is common to man. And God is faithful; he will not let you be tempted beyond what you can bear. But when you are tempted, he will also provide a way out so that you can stand up under it.

1 Corinthians 10:13 NIV

Many Christians, even pastors, do not believe it is possible to be free from lust. That isn't what the Bible says. The Psalmist teaches that a person's ways can be pure if he lives according to God's Word.

When you put scriptures on purity down into your spirit and heart, so that they automatically come out when Satan tempts you in the area of improper sexual desires, you can become free and pure.

There is also something else very practical you can do to reduce the possibility of lustfulness in your life: *Be careful what you allow into your mind and spirit!* Don't put yourself in the path of temptation. Avoid viewing risque movies or reading pornographic literature. Remember the motto of computer programmers: GIGO (*Garbage In, Garbage Out*)!

In 2 Corinthians 7:1 Paul urges us: "Since we have these promises, dear friends, let us purify ourselves from everything that contaminates body and spirit..."

If you have been involved in sexual sin (and as a result feel "contaminated" or defiled), today's prayer will take care of that problem.

The affirmation and scriptures I suggested two days ago can give you lasting, overcoming victory in this area.

Memorize that affirmation and at least three corresponding scripture verses, because you will be using them often against the temptation of lust. This is your "way out' which God has promised.

Prayer: "I praise You, heavenly Father, that You have forgiven my sins. I now ask You to cleanse me from the inside out with the energy of Jesus' blood. Take away all defilement from my spirit, heart, mind and body. Thank You that I am forgiven, cleansed and free. Help me to be faithful to renew my mind to firmly establish purity in my life.

"In Christ's Name, Amen."

Today's Scripture Reading: 1 Thessalonians 4:1-8, 5:19-24 (In *The Amplified Bible,* if possible)

Week 9 Day 7
Establishing Purity II

"Blessed are the pure in heart for they will see God."
Matthew 5:8 NIV

For years I read and quoted this verse thinking it meant that the pure in heart would one day get to go to heaven where they would see God with their physical eyes. It does mean this, of course. But then one day I suddenly realized that the verb "to see" has another meaning.

Consider the statement we often make, "Oh, now I *see*." Meaning, "I *comprehend*," or, "I *understand*."

We must have a pure heart (spirit) before we can fully know or understand God. Since He is perfectly pure, it is impossible for the impure person to have true knowledge of God or His ways. Satan does not want us to get to the place where we understand God's ways, so he strongly opposes us to keep us from having a pure and perfect heart.

In Matthew 5:48 (*NIV*), Jesus says to us: "Be perfect, therefore, as your heavenly Father is perfect."

In Philippians 1:10 (*NIV*), Paul prays that we may "be pure and blameless until the day of Christ."

If purity and perfection of heart were impossible, the Bible would not instruct us to possess them. It is not easy to attain these virtues, but it is possible! The perfect spirit and heart are attained through the cleansing power of Jesus' blood, and a pure thought life is possible through the application of God's Word.

Prayer: "Thank You, Father, for giving me a new and perfect spirit through the atoning blood of Jesus. Give me the perseverance within to use Your Word daily to defeat Satan and to renew my mind to purity of attitude and thought.

"In Christ's Name, Amen."

Today's Scripture Reading: Philippians 1:9-11, 2:12-16, 4:8

Week 10
Overcoming Overeating

Week 10 Day 1
Overcoming Overeating I

...God has given us an appetite for food and stomachs to digest it. But that doesn't mean we should eat more than we need.
1 Corinthians 6:13 TLB

There are many Christians in our churches who would never consider even drinking an alcoholic beverage much less getting drunk. Yet in these same churches there are many gluttons. It is interesting to note that each time gluttony is mentioned in the Bible, it is linked with drunkenness (Deut. 21:20; Prov. 23:21.) or winebibbing. (Matt. 11:19; Luke 7:34.)

Once again Satan has "come in the back door" with a less obvious sin (although the extra pounds caused by gluttony soon become quite obvious to everyone). Perhaps I should say that Satan comes in with a less-preached-against sin. Have you ever heard even one sermon against overeating? It is probably the least condemned of any sin.

Our church social times almost always center around food. The pot-luck dinner replete with mouth-watering and calorie-laden dishes (especially sweets!) has almost become the "trademark" of the Christian Church. Wherever two or three are gathered together, there is food. The temptation to overindulge is ever before us.

Many people were conditioned to overeat as children. In many homes food was used as a reward for good behavior or an an expression of parental love and approval. Some children were disciplined rather severely if they didn't "clean up their plate."

In most churches, Temperance Sunday was dedicated to talking about the evils of alcoholic drink. Yet we weren't taught to be temperate in *all* areas of our lives.

Many people need inner healing in this area of gluttony. If you are one of them, you can be delivered from overeating. Pray the suggested prayer and follow it up with the positive affirmation, putting appropriate scripture into your spirit, heart and mind.

Prayer: "Dear Lord, I come against Satan and all the rulers of darkness in this area of my life. I cast out the principalities and powers that are not of righteousness, and I establish a new inner government under the control of Jesus Christ. I confess that Jesus is giving me the self-control not to eat more than my body needs.

"I ask forgiveness for my sin of gluttony and overeating. I ask You, Lord, to heal any memories or hurts in the past that would cause an overeating problem. Help me to put food in its proper perspective. I thank and praise You for forgiveness, for healing and for new power. Jesus, You are Lord of my life.

"In Your Name I pray, Amen."

Today's Scripture Reading: Proverbs 23:1-21

Week 10 Day 2
Overcoming Overeating II

For the kingdom of God is not a matter of eating and drinking, but of righteousness, peace and joy in the Holy Spirit.
Romans 14:17 NIV

For many people, food has become a substitute or false "cure" because they don't have inner peace and joy. They overeat in a futile attempt to fill the void they feel on the inside. For such people, as well as for you and me, this verse contains the key to filling that inner void!

In the past, your attempts at dieting have no doubt been based on gaining physical (and perhaps mental) control over your body. But in so doing, you have neglected the root cause of your problem — your spirit or heart.

The correct way to take dominion over your physical body and mind is to first get your spirit healed and under God's control. Then you can go on to disciplining your heart (with the help of God's Word) to take authority and control over your body.

Very often Derin and I receive letters from desperate overweight people who are crying out for help. If you are plagued with this problem of overeating, I believe this week's devotionals will give you spiritual and practical help to lose weight sensibly and keep it off. (If you are not overweight or do not have any problem with food, you can use these devotionals to learn how to help others in this area.)

What must be done to gain control over our lives in all areas, including eating, is to establish the righteousness, peace and joy of the kingdom of God within our spirit and heart, though the power of the Holy Spirit.

When righteousness is established in our hearts and lives, then peace and joy are the results we begin to see, because peace and joy are two of the fruits of the Spirit of God. (Gal. 5:22,23.) Another one of these fruits is temperance (which *The New International Version* translates as *self-control*). ALL of the fruits of the Spirit are to be evident in the Christian's life. The Word of God says we believers will be known by our fruit. (Luke 6:44.) And the way to produce fruit is to first plant a seed — the seed of the Word!

Prayer: "Dear Lord, in the Name of Jesus, I cast down gluttony and intemperance. I establish self-control, self-restraint and temperance in my life. With Your help, I will break the habit of overeating and gluttony.

"Help me to live a righteous, Spirit-controlled life. May the fruits of peace and joy and self-control develop in my inner being so I have no compulsion to eat more than I need. 'I have hidden your word in my heart that I might not sin against you' " (Ps. 119:11 *NIV*).

"In Jesus' Name, Amen."

Today's Scripture Reading: Galatians 5

Week 10 Day 3
Overcoming Overeating III

Jesus answered, "It is written: 'Man does not live on bread alone, but on every word that comes from the mouth of God.'"

Matthew 4:4 NIV

Once overeating has become an ingrained habit, it is very difficult to break out of the "gluttony pattern." All those people who, through great difficulty and self-discipline, have lost many pounds only to put them right back on again, can attest to this fact!

This "off-again, on-again" habit pattern can be broken through the power of the Word of God. Although Christ had been without food for 40 days in the wilderness, He was able to resist Satan's temptation to turn stones to bread. He did it by quoting scripture. (Luke 4:1-4.) If our Lord could do that, then surely we can resist eating food we don't even need by using that same Word.

Today's scripture, quoted aloud, is a strong deterrent to the temptation to eat something we know we shouldn't.

Memorized scriptures, along with today's affirmation, will help you break the overeating habit in your life.

Prayer: "Father, I praise You that You are giving me overcoming power in the area of overeating.

"I ask that You bless my body with correct metabolism to properly assimilate and make use of what I eat. Help me to be able to visualize myself, in faith, as a slender, attractive person.

"I know that my body is the temple of Your Holy Spirit; may it bring glory to You. Help me to care for my body in the proper way.

"In Jesus' Name, Amen."

Today's Scripture Reading: 2 Corinthians 4 (NIV)

Affirmation: "I yield control of my appetite and eating habits to Christ. I do not eat more than my body needs."

Affirmation Scriptures (Choose at least three of the following scriptures and memorize them to use against temptation each day, as often as needed, until you are at your ideal weight): *Matthew 4:4, 6:25b; Luke 12:29; Romans 8:1 (AMP), 14:17; 1 Corinthians 10:23,31.*

Week 10 Day 4
Overcoming Overeating IV

"And do not set your heart on what you will eat or drink..."
Luke 12:29 NIV

When we "set our heart" on food, we are giving too much importance to eating. Do you "eat to live" or "live to eat"? For many people, food is a time- and emotion-consuming thing. Check to see how much of your time is spent thinking and talking about food — how much time is devoted to actually eating.

Our social structure often centers around food — family gatherings, special days, eating out. I'm somewhat amused that almost every woman's magazine in America contains, in the very same issue, the latest and "best-ever" diet for losing weight, right along with tempting recipes and mouth-watering pictures of fattening food. No wonder most dieters are on a "yo-yo" diet — their scales go up and down like a yo-yo as the pounds go on and off and back on again!

The average dieter has probably "lost" hundreds of pounds — the only trouble is he has gained back the same amount — or more! The percentage of overweight people who take off pounds and keep them off is very low. Obviously people need more than a crash diet. They need a change that goes deeper than that. They need to replace old habits with new ones.

Through the prayer example given on Day 2 of this week — and through using God's Word for the renewing of your mind — you can change your habits in the area of eating.

Whenever you are tempted to overeat, defeat Satan by making scripturally-based affirmations. For example: "My body is the temple of the Holy Spirit. I do not eat more than it needs. My heart is not set on what I eat, because the kingdom of God is not a matter of eating and drinking, but of righteousness, peace and joy in the Holy Spirit. I do not live according to the dictates of my flesh, but according to the dictates of the Spirit."

Prayer: "Father, I praise You that Your Word is alive in me, giving me self-control in the area of eating. I praise You for helping me keep my heart set on You. Amen."

Today's Scripture Reading: Luke 12:22-34

Week 10 Day 5
Overcoming Overeating V

So whether you eat or drink or whatever you do, do it all for the glory of God.

1 Corinthians 10:31 NIV

Recently I read a story about a girl with anorexia nervosa. An excerpt printed in conjunction with the article provided some interesting facts. This psychological illness which causes people to destroy their bodies through excessive "dieting" has increased 1,000% in the past five years. This proves that a person does not have to be overweight to have an incorrect view of eating. Many thin people are also "hung up" on food.

As Christians we should be aware of proper nutrition and be careful to eat the kinds of food that are good for our bodies. If we desire to walk in divine health, we cannot expect to do so only through confession of health scriptures. We must also pay attention to correct eating habits and proper exercise and rest.

Remember that your body is the temple of the Holy Spirit. In the Old Testament, God gave very detailed instructions about the proper care and maintenance of the temple. God's dwelling place was extremely beautiful and the people were cautioned never to defile it.

I believe God is still particular about His temple (our bodies) today. I believe He desires that it be a credit to the One who indwells it, that it bring glory to Him. In that sense, each of us is charged with the sober responsibility of "temple guard."

Prayer: "Father, I ask that You direct me and give me the self-discipline to care for Your temple correctly. May all I do be to Your glory.

"In Christ's Name, Amen."

Today's Scripture Reading: Psalm 119:73-96

Week 10 Day 6
Overcoming Overeating VI

Is not life greater [in quality] than food...?
Matthew 6:25 AMP

What I desire to see you achieve through this study is a certain *quality* of life. A life in which your spirit, in obedience to God's Holy Spirit, is in control of your body.

It seems, however, that to bring the body into proper perspective, we must not only make positive affirmations and repeat scriptures, we must discipline the body by exercising it regularly and by cutting down on our intake of calories.

If a person only reduces his food intake, the body eventually "adjusts" to getting by on a smaller amount. His metabolism slows down and his weight may stay at a certain place even though he has cut back drastically on the amount he eats.

To combat this problem of decreased metabolism, you need to exercise at least 12 to 15 minutes a day. I suggest one mile of fast walking or jogging or a quarter-hour of dancing to lively praise music.

In addition (not instead of!), you should talk to your body. Tell its metabolism to function correctly; command it to lose weight.

Here are some daily affirmations I use to gain control over my physical body:

"The food I eat goes to energy and strength, not to fat.

"I am a slender person. It is easy for me to lose weight. My body's metabolism works perfectly.

"I do not eat more than my body needs.

"I do not easily gain back the weight I have lost. I am a slim and attractive person.

"I do not live according to the dictates of my flesh, but according to the dictates of the Holy Spirit. (Rom. 8:1 AMP.)"

Prayer: "Dear Lord, please bless my body with correct metabolism and hormonal balance. Help me to have self-control so as not to eat more than I need. Help me to eat the right kinds of food. Please bless me with the self-discipline to exercise regularly. I set my will to be disciplined in my physical habits.

"In Jesus' Name, Amen."

Today's Scripture Reading: Matthew 6:25-34

Week 10 Day 7
Overcoming Overeating VII

...live not after the dictates of the flesh, but after the dictates of the Spirit.

Romans 8:1 AMP

In my endeavors to lose weight, I believe this is the verse that has been the most helpful to me. Overeating was, to me, giving into the dictates of my flesh, or body. Then I learned that having God direct my eating — being able to say "no" to food I didn't really need — was truly living by the Spirit's dictates, or in the Spirit's control. (Note: The word "Spirit" in this verse is capitalized, so it refers to God's Holy Spirit.)

I was pleased that when I was tempted to eat a piece of candy or other unnecessary food item, this verse would come into my mind and out of my mouth. (It helps to say verses *aloud* when tempted.)

The "way out" when tempted (which Paul mentions in 1 Corinthians 10:13 *NIV*) is to speak the Word. In Matthew 4:1-11, Jesus used the Word of God against Satan to resist his temptations. As a result, Satan left Him alone and angels came to minister to Him.

When we speak the Word, we are resisting Satan in the most effective way available to us. As we do, he will flee from us as the scripture says. (James 4:7.) So when the devil comes and tempts you to overeat or to eat incorrectly (too much, too little or the wrong things), defeat him by quoting Romans 8:1. It is short and to the point and easily memorized!

You no longer need to be ruled by your fleshly appetite, but you can be under the control of the Holy Spirit within you!

Prayer: "Dear Father, this day I choose to be controlled by Your Holy Spirit in all areas of my life, especially in the area of food and eating habits. I will walk in Your precepts and commands, and will allow the Holy Spirit to control my mouth — both what goes into it and what comes out of it.

"Help me to be strong in this commitment and to stand fast (persevere) until good eating habits are established in my life.

"In the strong Name of Jesus, Amen."

Today's Scripture Reading: Romans 8:1-14 (in *The Amplified Bible*, if possible)

For further teaching of spiritual insights into correct eating, I recommend *The Diet Alternative*, by Diane Hampton. Publisher Whitaker House. Copyright 1984.

Week 11
Knowing God's Provision

Week 11 Day 1
God's Love

How great is the love the Father has lavished on us, that we should be called children of God!

1 John 3:1 NIV

God loves you. Nothing you have done or will ever do can diminish His boundless love in any way. If we could only realize and understand His love, our lives would never be the same!

If you have an unsaved relative or friend about whom you are concerned, pray that Satan will no longer be able to blind him to God's love and mercy. Because, you see, if that person knew how much God really loves him, he would quickly turn to Him and receive that love. Pray also that the Lord will send loving people into his life so that God's love will be revealed to him through them.

You know how you desire to give good gifts to your children, how you want the best for their lives. So very much more does Your heavenly Father desire good for His children! (Matt. 7:11.)

You may be wondering, ''Then why don't I see more good things in my life than I do?'' There are two reasons. One is because there are so many evil influences in today's world, so much unbelief, so much doubt about what God's will is, so much questioning about the Bible. Secondly, what God says in Hosea 4:6 is true: ''My people are destroyed for lack of knowledge.''

Over and over we find that people are ignorant about what the Word of God has to say about health, money and God's ways in most areas of life. The only part of the scriptures most people know is the message of salvation, therefore salvation is all they have. It is good that they have that, because it is the most important and the most eternal of God's blessings. But God longs for His children to know about and receive *all* He has provided for them through Jesus Christ. In 3 John 2, He says to us through the Apostle John: "Beloved, I pray that you may prosper *in every way* and [that your body] may keep well, even as [I know] your soul keeps well and prospers" (*AMP*).

Are you prospering "in every way"? If not, pray this prayer in sincerity and faith.

Prayer: "Dear Father, please break through my mental blocks and reveal to my spirit Your great love for me. As nearly as possible with my human mind, may I understand Your infinite love towards me and all people everywhere. Help me to return love to You freely and to enjoy close companionship and fellowship with You daily. Show me how to avail myself of every blessing which is mine as Your beloved child. I worship, praise and thank You, Lord.

"In Jesus' Name, Amen."

Today's Scripture Reading: 1 John 2:28—3:24

Week 11 Day 2
God's Comfort

"...I will turn their mourning into gladness; I will give them comfort and joy instead of sorrow."

Jeremiah 31:13 NIV

Recently I counseled a lady who was still carrying deep grief over the death of her little boy which had occurred over 20 years ago. She told me she had not slept since he died. If only someone had shared with this lady how to give her grief to God, she could have been spared all those years of unhappiness!

As we talked together, I was able to show her how to allow forgiveness to flow through her to her husband and the doctor (both of whom she blamed for the death), and then to God (against whom she harbored bitterness for "allowing" such a tragedy to happen).

Of course, there is sorrow when a loved one dies. I experienced deep sorrow when my mother passed away.

But I gave that inconsolable grief over to Jesus, because He came to carry my sorrows for me (Is. 53:4), and to bind up the brokenhearted and to comfort all who mourn. (Is. 61:1,2.)

I did not have to bear unnecessary grief because I allowed God to comfort me, and He still is helping me.

There can be comfort and peace — (yes, even a quiet sense of joy) — deep down in your spirit even when your heart is sorrowing. This comfort comes by allowing God to heal your heart. The Psalmist said of God: ''The Lord is close to the brokenhearted and saves those who are crushed in spirit'' (Ps. 34:18 *NIV*).

Derin and I have ministered this comfort to parents whose children were killed in accidents, and it has helped them greatly.

(One word of caution: *Give the grieving person some time.* For a while after the death of someone very close to them, people are often in a state of shock, not really comprehending the tragedy which has befallen them. After this period of shock has passed, the prayer for healing and the scriptures on comfort can be shared. Please be very sensitive to the leading of the Holy Spirit in this area!)

Prayer (For yourself or to minister comfort to the grief-stricken): **''Dear Lord, I yield to You my hurt, grief and sorrow. I do not understand this tragedy, but I know Your *perfect* will can not always be done here on earth. I know You sent Jesus to heal the brokenhearted, and I accept that healing right now. Please take away the grief in my spirit and heart and replace it with Your comfort and peace.**

''In Jesus' Name, Amen.''

Today's Scripture Reading: Isaiah 61:1-3

Affirmation: ''Lord, I give to You all the hurt, sorrow and grief in my life. I thank You that I no longer have to carry them because Jesus carried them for me.''

Affirmation Scriptures: Nehemiah 8:10; Psalm 119:76; Isaiah 25:8, 26:19, 53:3,4, 60:20, 61:1-3, 66:13; Matthew 5:4; John 14:1-3, 16:20,22; 1 Corinthians 15:54; 2 Corinthians 1:3; 2 Thessalonians 2:16,17 (AMP).

Week 11 Day 3
God's Protection

The Lord will keep you from all harm — he will watch over your life; the Lord will watch over your coming and going both now and forevermore.

Psalm 121:7,8 NIV

The Bible uses an interesting metaphor to illustrate God's protection of us: "He will cover you with his feathers, and under his wings you will find refuge..." (Ps. 91:4 *NIV*). The Psalmist David cried out to God: "...in the shadow of Your wings will I rejoice" (Ps. 63:7 *AMP*). And in Luke 13:34 Jesus said He longed to gather Jerusalem's children together "as a hen gathers her chicks under her wings" (*NIV*).

This likening of God to a mother hen is not just imaginative imagery. The Bible has many "hidden meanings," and this is one good example. It is my understanding that the chicken is one of the few creatures in all the animal kingdom that will stay with her young and protect them with her very life. In a prairie fire, the mother hen will gather her little chicks under her wings and will burn to death protecting them rather than run away from the fire as other animals do.

So, in these scriptures, God is illustrating and emphasizing how strong and sure is His protection over us. When you establish this assurance of protection in your spirit, you can eliminate much fear from your life.

"Are not all angels ministering spirits sent to serve those who will inherit salvation?" (Heb. 1:14 *NIV*). Angels were created to help and protect us believers. Use them! Each day thank God that He has given His angels charge over you to keep you in all your ways (Ps. 91:11.), and for the assurance of your family's safety. In 1 Corinthians 4:15 Paul tells us that we have "ten thousand guardians in Christ." Are you availing yourself of the full protection of all these personal body guards? If not, there is a lot of "angel power" going to waste!

Prayer: "Father, I thank You for Your loving presence which surrounds me. Thank You for Your angels who are

my guardians to keep me from harm. Help me to learn about Your protection and to appropriate it in my life. "In Jesus' Name, Amen."

Daily Scripture Reading: Psalm 91

Affirmation: "Each day God's presence and protection surrounds my family and me."

Affirmation Scriptures: Psalm 5:12, 4:8, 40:11, 36:6,7, 1:6, 55:22, 91:11; Isaiah 63:9; Proverbs 18:10, 28:18; Hebrews 1:14; Psalm 34:7, 40:11, 63:7, 102:28 (AMP).

Week 11 Day 4
God's Strength

"For the eyes of the Lord range throughout the earth to strengthen those whose hearts are fully committed to him..."
2 Chronicles 16:9 NIV

God desires to help us, to protect us, to empower us. Because we are His beloved children, it is His will to give us strength for daily living. We receive this strength by confessing His Word.

Do you ever have one of those days when you are already tired before you even begin your day's work? Doesn't that usually happen the very day you have a multitude of things to do? Well, I have those days myself from time to time. But I have learned how to handle them — and it works!

Before I ever start my day, I confess that I have God's strength. Then I say some Bible verses which I have memorized on the subject of strength. All through the day I continue to affirm strength and to repeat those verses. At the end of the day I find that my work is all done — and I still have strength left over. It's great!

Another reason you will have added energy as you walk in the ways of God is because you will not be draining away your strength through anger, guilt, frustration and fear. Negative emotions sap energy. Mental distress can be very tiring. Holding a grudge against someone is hard work. Depression can make you feel like doing absolutely nothing!

115

As you walk more and more in the Word, you will become more and more congruent in spirit, mind and body. You will find that harmony and wholeness add vitality to your life.

In Joel 3:10 God says, "Let the weak say, I am strong." God's Word is truth. When you speak it, you are confessing truth, whether that is the way you *feel* right at that moment or not. Remember: The truth is not dependent upon our feelings!

Prayer: "Dear Lord, I thank You for giving me strength in my spirit to walk in Your way, strength in my mind to meditate on Your Word and have right attitudes, and strength in my body to do my daily tasks as unto the Lord.

"In Jesus' Name, Amen."

Today's Scripture Reading: Isaiah 40:28-31

Affirmation: "Jesus gives me strength for every situation."

Affirmation Scriptures (There are many good verses concerning strength. Memorize and use them whenever needed.): *Philippians 4:13; Ephesians 3:16; Colossians 1:11; Isaiah 40:29-31, 58:11; Psalm 73:26, 46:1, 18:32; Nehemiah 8:10; Deuteronomy 33:25; Zechariah 10:12.*

Week 11 Day 5
God's Mercy

O give thanks to the Lord for He is good, for His mercy and lovingkindness endure for ever!

Psalm 107:1 AMP

Because of His great love for us, God has much mercy on us. That is a message many Christians need to hear. If you were brought up as I was, you heard many sermons about the judgments of God, but not too many about His mercy.

Our church (but, thank God, not my parents!) taught what I call the doctrine of "eternal insecurity." Their belief seemed to be that a person could live a godly life for years and years, but if he wasn't careful he could commit some sin before he died — and wake up in hell! Understandably, with that kind of outlook most of the members of that church lived in constant fear of "falling from grace," of coming under condemnation from God.

I had a relative who lived in sin and rebellion against God for many years. Yet God, in His loving mercy, forgave that man and he was saved the night before he died and so is now in heaven.

Our God of love *always* desires good for us. But our willful disobedience, our disregard of His ways, our lack of knowledge of His will can keep us from experiencing all the good things He has in store for us. Psalm 136:23 assures us that our loving heavenly Father has "[earnestly] remembered us in our low state and imprinted us [on his heart], for his mercy and loving-kindness endure for ever" (*AMP*).

Jesus, our High Priest, is in heaven right now interceding for us with the Father. (Heb. 7:25.) As our substitute, He became the perfect sacrifice for our sins to make it possible for God to forgive us, to extend mercy to us instead of judgment. And, of course, it was God's own love that caused Him to send Jesus to earth to become sin for us (though He Himself was sinless) in order to redeem us from all sin and condemnation. (2 Cor. 5:21; Rom. 8:1.)

Prayer: "Thank You, Father, for Your mercy to me and to all people. Please enlighten the eyes of my spirit and heart so I may better understand and appreciate Your great love and mercy.

"In Jesus' Name, Amen."

Today's Scripture Reading: Psalm 118

Week 11 Day 6
God's Goodness

How great is your goodness, which you have stored up for those who fear you, which you bestow in the sight of men on those who take refuge in you.

Psalm 31:19 NIV

God is love. (1 John 4:16.) His acts toward us are based in love. He always desires to do good for us. Why then do we not see more good happening in this world? Because there are certain things that we, the followers of Jesus, must do so that God can freely work.

In her book, *The Healing Gifts of the Spirit*, Agnes Sanford says: ''(Some) people ignore the fact that while undoubtedly all things are possible with God, all things are not as yet possible with them. Their power is not as yet developed nor is their faith stabilized. They forget also that God does not work through magic, but through the application of laws and of powers He has created;...they do not realize that no one lives alone and the entire race must rise to a higher awareness of God before all things that are possible with God become actual.''*

Water flows downhill. But it can be stopped with a dam. God's goodness always flows toward us. But it can be stopped by ignorance, disbelief, bitterness, sin (and its resulting guilt) and by fear.

All of these blockages can be removed from your life through prayer and faithful application of the Word of God. After they are removed and you are whole in spirit, mind and body, then you can be instrumental in the healing of your family, friends, church, city and even the whole earth.

This freedom is not easy to obtain or maintain. It demands the self-discipline to set aside an hour or two each day to pray and study the Bible. It requires the consistent and repeated application of scriptural truths each day to break any strongholds of Satan in your life. Those strongholds were not established instantaneously, and usually they will not be destroyed instantaneously. It takes time and effort to totally eradicate them. But it is well worth it!

Because my husband and I have chosen to live this way, we have seen ourselves, our marriage and our family healed. And as a result of our own personal spiritual liberation, we

Revell, Old Tappen, New Jersey, copyright (no date), p. 49.

have been able to help thousands of other people to become free in their spirits.

Prayer: "Thank You, Father, for Your great goodness! Help me to be aligned with Your Word so it can flow to me and through me to others.

"In Jesus' Name, Amen."

Today's Scripture Reading: Psalm 107

Week 11 Day 7
God's Grace

For all have sinned and fall short of the glory of God, and are justified freely by his grace through the redemption that came by Christ Jesus.

Romans 3:23,24 NIV

If we truly understood God's grace and the redemption that He provided for us through Jesus, how different our lives would be! Condemnation of fellow-Christians would be gone. We would work to encourage each other and to build each other up.

If we would realize that God's grace has made us guiltless before Him, then we would have no need to point out other people's sins in an effort to justify our own.

The false guilt of our past sins would be gone because we would realize that the grace of God has erased them completely through the blood of His Son, Jesus.

We could still the accuser, Satan, if we would understand that our redemption enables us to stand before God with no fear, guilt or condemnation, because God's grace, through Jesus, has made us as though we had never sinned.

We would understand that we are to have dominion and power to reign here on earth. In Romans 5:17 Paul tells us: "...how much more will those who receive God's abundant provision of grace and of the gift of righteousness reign in life through the one man, Jesus Christ" (*NIV*).

Those who preach condemnation also preach "coping." The Word of God does not say that we are "copers" but that we are more than *conquerors* through Jesus Christ, that we reign in life through Him! (Rom. 8:37, 5:17.)

No doubt, the "copers" will be in heaven too, but how much better is life here on earth when we know we are ruling and reigning as kings and priests! (Rev. 1:6.) Sin is so longer our master for we are not under the law, but under *grace*. (Rom. 6:14.)

Prayer: "Dear Lord, thank You for Your gift of grace. Help me to understand it more fully, so I may be free in You and understand my scriptural identity.
"In Jesus' Name, Amen."

Today's Scripture Reading: Romans 5

Affirmation: "Because of God's grace, I stand before Him with no fear, guilt or condemnation."

Affirmation Scriptures: Ephesians 2:4-10; Romans 3:23,24, 8:37, 5:17,20,21, 6:14; 2 Corinthians 8:9; Galatians 2:21; Revelation 1:6.

Week 12
Marital Relationships

Week 12 Day 1
The Spirit of Marriage

*Has not the Lord made them one? In flesh and spirit they
are his. And why one? Because he was seeking godly offspring.
So guard yourself in your spirit, and do not break faith with the
wife of your youth.*

Malachi 2:15 NIV

In the last book of the Old Testament, we find this
admonition from the Lord to His people. He stresses the
importance of a godly marriage — what would today be a
Christ-centered, Spirit-controlled marriage.

Twice this scripture emphasizes the importance of
guarding the spirit within, of a husband and wife not breaking faith with each other.

Physical unfaithfulness — adultery — is not the only
way to break faith. Perhaps an even more devastating way
of breaking faith in a marriage is through injury to the spirit
of the marriage.

Love is the spirit, the basis of marriage. True love is
based on unselfishness, wanting good for our spouse more
than our own good. Another characteristic of this kind of
love is unconditional forgiveness. Unselfishness, forgiveness
— these attributes of real love are not possible without God's
Spirit being within us.

Our society places much importance on physical compatibility in marriage — good sexual adjustment, ability to
talk out problems and agreement in financial matters.
Obviously, all the books and articles written to help couples
in these areas have not cured the basic problems, otherwise
our divorce rate in the United States would not be almost
50%.

The spirit of a marriage is *so* much more important than physical compatibility. Yet most of the marriage "experts" do not even know it exists! If both husband and wife will yield themselves to the Holy Spirit and confess their wrong attitudes in the spiritual realm of their marriage, refusing to speak negatively about their marriage and spouse, renewing their minds with positive affirmations, I believe there is no problem in their marriage that cannot be solved — no matter how long-standing or seemingly unsolvable it may be.

The Christian marriage is to be an example to the world of God's love — how it really works in everyday life. Lately, especially, the Christian witness has been falling apart as more and more "Christian" marriages break up.

In this week's devotionals you will find the "how-to's," the ways to get your marriage on the right track. If you will do what these devotionals suggest, you will see almost miraculous changes in your marriage — even if your spouse is not a Christian, your marriage can be healed.

In the middle of Malachi 2:15 a question is asked: "And why one in flesh and spirit?" Then that question is answered: "Because he was seeking godly offspring." God wanted our children to be His and to serve Him. That is one reason, if not the main reason, a Christian marriage is so important. Next week's devotionals will go into detail on how to bring up your children according to God's ways.

Prayer: "Father, I come to You in the Name of Jesus, Your Son. I ask forgiveness for the times I have been selfish, unforgiving, inconsiderate and hostile in my marriage. (If you have been physically unfaithful in your marriage, ask forgiveness for that also.) **My actions of the past have wounded _____'s spirit and damaged the oneness of spirit that should be in our marriage. I repent of these acts and attitudes that have 'broken the faith' of our marriage. I determine to turn away from them.**

"From now on, I will seek Your wisdom in our marriage. I will show consideration, compassion, love and forgiveness in our day-to-day relationship.

"Father, I am now ready to forgive _____ for everything that he/she has ever done to hurt me in any way. I ask for Your divine forgiveness to flow from Jesus and then through me to him/her. I forgive _____ and release him/her right now.

"I rebuke and cancel all negative words I have ever said about _____ or our marriage. I say that they can no longer operate against us or our home in any way. I ask that You put a watch on my mouth that I never again say negative things against _____ or our marriage.

"I now bless _____ with the love and light of Christ and with spiritual growth. I bless our marriage with a spirit of love and forgiveness. I bless both of us, in Jesus' Name, with assurance that we are loved and accepted by the other one. I ask that the spirit of our marriage be totally healed.

"In Jesus' Name, Amen."

Today's Scripture Reading: Malachi 2:13—3:5

Week 12 Day 2
Forgiveness in Your Marriage

Bear with each other and forgive whatever grievances you may have against one another. Forgive as the Lord forgave you.
Colossians 3:13 NIV

Forgiveness is a basic ingredient in love. Unforgiveness blocks love. It also blocks communication with God. Do you have any unanswered prayers? Instead of asking, "Why doesn't God answer my prayers?", check out why the Lord may not *be able* to answer them. Unforgiveness of others or yourself or anger toward God may be the reason.

In the marriage relationship, unforgiveness also blocks communication. If your spouse does not do what you want or ask, check to make sure that the problem is not unforgiveness on your part. Your mate may be held in bondage by unforgiveness, causing him or her to resist you — perhaps not consciously, but subconsciously.

A spirit held in bondage is not free to love freely and completely, as I learned in my own marriage. As long as I felt my husband was "demanding" that I love him, I found it difficult to do so. As a Christian, desiring to do right and to be a good wife, I prayed that I would love him and tried to love him, but that didn't really work.

When Derin became free, when he forgave me and was willing to let me love him as I would — then love came flowing in. Our marriage was resurrected. Love grew without struggle. My spirit was released and I became free to give and receive love — and that is exactly what I did. Praise the Lord!

I used to have a certain amount of fear of my husband. Sometimes I did things I really would have preferred not to do, simply because I feared angering my husband. The Bible say, "Perfect love drives out fear" (1 John 4:18a *NIV*). I can testify that this is true. When husband and wife have perfect love, there is no fear in their relationship.

Be willing to forgive — not only past hurts, but things that come up in the course of day-to-day living. Forgiveness will heal a hurting marriage. It will strengthen a good marriage, making it even better.

Prayer: "Father, I praise You that I have already forgiven _____, that I have allowed Your divine forgiveness to flow through me to him/her. I bless both of us with a continued spirit of forgiveness that we will never again hold each other in bondage with an attitude of unforgiveness. I thank You for peace in our home.
"In Christ's Name, Amen."

Today's Scripture Reading: Colossians 3:12-21

Week 12 Day 3
Love Your Husband

...train the...women to love their husbands and children, to be self-controlled and pure, to be busy at home, to be kind, and to be subject to their husbands...

Titus 2:4,5 NIV

There are other passages in the Bible which mention that the wife should be subject to, or submitted to, her husband. (Eph. 5:24; 1 Tim. 2:11-15; Col. 3:18.) Some people have a problem accepting this teaching. You may be one of them. If so, take time to study the cultures of the world which are characterized by matriarchal dominance as opposed to patriarchal dominance. I believe you will soon conclude that such societies are not nearly as strong, inventive or industrious as those in which the father is recognized as the head of the home. I wonder how long it will take mankind to understand that God's ways are right and best!

In the first years of my marriage, I did not desire to be submissive, neither did I understand this Biblical principle. As a result, Derin and I went through several years of problems, hurts, anger and bitterness. Probably the only thing that kept us together was our strong Christian heritage and upbringing.

Then about nine years ago, I asked the Holy Spirit into my life. In yielding myself to Him, I opened the way for God to start changing me into the kind of wife and mother I should be. It was a gradual change as I learned to yield my will and rights to God as He convicted me. Now I have an attitude of submission, and our marriage is better in every way.

As a wife, you should understand that when I speak of your being subject to your husband, I do not mean to imply granting him a license to become a "tyrant" in the family. I am not advocating subservience, but rather an attitude of love and proper respect which opens up a channel for God to work through your marriage to bring about changes in *both of you*. In my own experience, I discovered that godly "submission" on my part actually made me a freer person than when I was trying to "do my own thing" — and produced a much better climate for the happy and fulfilling marriage I really desired.

This may not sound possible to you, but I assure you that it has been so in my marriage. I do not have to manipulate my husband to get my way; because of my attitude and behavior toward him, he *gives* me my way. He

125

has a desire to do things that please me. He is more considerate, kind and loving — and I am happier and more secure.

If you are a wife of a non-Christian husband, you may be thinking, "This won't work in my marriage, because my husband is not saved." But notice what the Apostle Peter has to say about this subject: "Wives, in the same way be submissive to your husbands so that, if any of them do not believe the word, they may be won over without talk by the *behavior* of their wives, when they see the *purity* and *reverence* of your lives" (1 Pet. 3:1,2 *NIV*).

God's ways work. When we are in line with them, He is able to bring about His will in our marriage. It is God's will that your husband come to Him. Start today by praying that your spouse will develop a thirst for righteousness and a desire to know God.

Prayer: "Father, I come to You in the Name of Jesus Christ, Your Son. I confess that You will give me a spirit of love and submissiveness in my marriage. I repent of any wrong attitudes and words of the past, and I bind Satan from acting on them to injure the spirit of our marriage. I bless _____ with Your wisdom and guidance. I bless him with a thirst for righteousness and a desire to love and serve You. In faith, I say he is the spiritual leader of our home. I yield my will to You. In our marriage I set my will to follow Your ways as taught in the Bible.

"In the Name of Jesus, Amen."

Today's Scripture Reading: 1 Timothy 2:11-15

Affirmation: "I love _____ and submit myself to him as to the Lord. He is my provider and security. I support his decisions. _____ loves me as Christ loved the Church."

Affirmation Scriptures: 1 Peter 3:1-6; Titus 2:3-5; Ephesians 5:24; Colossians 3:18; Song of Solomon 2:4, 7:10.

Week 12 Day 4
The Godly Wife

Wives, submit to your husbands, as is fitting in the Lord.
Colossians 3:18 NIV

You may feel that yesterday's affirmation of submission to your husband is impossible. Remember what Romans 4:17 tells us about calling things that are not as though they were! Even though your husband may not be your provider and security at this time, if you continue to affirm and believe that he is, eventually he will become what you say he is. How? Through the power of God's Word. It is God's will (as stated in His Word) that your husband provide for you and make you secure. Since God has promised to watch over His Word to perform it (Jer. 1:12 *NIV.*), when you speak forth His Word in love and faith, God Himself will see to it that it becomes reality in your life.

I realize that your husband has his own will and can set it against God and His ways, but I believe that through prayer, fasting and confession of the Word you can do much to bind Satan's influence over your husband so he will be free to choose God's ways.

When you allow your husband to make the decisions in your home, in accordance with the plan and will of God, then you put the correct kind of "pressure" on him. God is able to guide and correct him in the area of decision-making. When your husband can not place any blame on you for wrong decisions, he becomes more aware of his great responsibility to make better and wiser decisions. This will actually work more to your advantage than if you tried to sway your husband through your own power.

If you have already come to the place where you don't love your husband any more, or are not sure you love him, or wish you didn't love him, this situation and attitude will be changed.

One basic need in the life of any wife is security. When this security is provided, love for the one who provides it naturally follows. Especially when the reason the husband makes her feel secure is because he loves her and desires the best for her. Which is how your husband will come to feel about you when you are a God-directed wife.

Your honest reaction to all this might be, "That all sounds good. But you don't know my husband. It would

take a miracle to ever get him to desire the best for me!"
Yes, it probably will take a miracle. But our God is a miracle-
working God. He has performed millions of them in the
past; one more won't be any problem to Him. What it takes
is for you to get in line with His ways.

Yesterday's verses say that a wife should be self-
controlled, pure, busy at home, and kind.

Self-controlled and busy at home — these two can be
looked at together. This may mean the self-control to turn
off the TV and clean house or do laundry. It may mean
dieting and exercising so that your body is more nearly like
the one that attracted your husband during courtship. Being
busy at home may mean saying "no" to some committee
work, clubs, lunches out with the girls, or even to some
of your church jobs. When any husband comes home from
work day after day to a fat, lazy wife and a dirty, unkept
house, no one can blame him for "losing his love"!

A pure wife has sexual desires directed only to her husband. She is not having an affair on the side with a boss,
friend or co-worker, nor does she feel she has to prove her
sexual attractiveness by flirting with other men.

Kindness is goodness in action, an attitude of heart that
is caring. It means not saying hurting, harsh words, but
rather being careful to do and say things that provide for
the other person's happiness before your own.

Through God's strength and the application of His
Word, you can be the kind of wife the Lord — and your
husband — desires for you to be.

**Prayer: "Dear Father, please reveal to me how to pray
correctly for my husband and our marriage. Give me the
wisdom and self-discipline I need to be a virtuous wife.
I choose to walk in Your ways in our marriage.**

"In Jesus' Name, Amen."

Today's Scripture Reading: Proverbs 31:10-31

Week 12 Day 5
Your Husband's Crown
A wife of noble character is her husband's crown.

Proverbs 12:4a NIV

Wife, don't think I'm "picking" on you! I'll be writing some things for your husband soon!

From all I've said thus far, you may be thinking, "This is not fair. I'm the one who is supposed to do all the giving in and changing." Your reasoning is logical and sound — from the world's point of view. A few years ago I would have no doubt felt the same way. But since then I have discovered a "better way." It is a way based on the teachings of the Bible.

When we, as wives, forgive and release our husbands and submit ourselves to them, we remove the blockage we've formerly been between them and God. This allows the Lord to have direct access to our husbands to change them into the kind of marriage partners He wants them to be. (You know, it is even possible that *all* the problems in your marriage aren't your husband's fault alone!)

I once counseled a beautiful Christian wife. From what she told me, I thought, "Wow! This lady's husband must really be a dud!" But later when I met the man, I found him to be a delightful and intelligent person. As I got to know that couple better, I concluded that it was the wife who was causing much of the husband's "misbehavior" through her strong spirit of manipulation and her selfishness.

Even if your husband is not a Christian, your being a wife of "noble character" will have a great effect on your marriage. The Apostle Peter says that husbands will be "won over" when they see the reverence and the purity of their Christian wives' behavior. (1 Pet. 3:1.)

How can you be this kind of wife? By confessing God's Word and affirming the characteristics which develop noble character.

These characteristics are: l) inner beauty (1 Pet. 3:3-6.), 2) self-control (Week 3), 3) a forgiving spirit (Week 1), 4) a good self-concept (Week 5), and 5) unselfishness (1 Cor. 13.).

When you become a wife of noble character, you put yourself in line with the Word of God. Then you can expect

His promise in Proverbs 31:28 to come true in your marriage: "Her children arise and call her blessed; her husband also, and he praises her" (*NIV*).

Prayer: "Father, I praise You that in Jesus' Name and for His glory You are making me into a wife of noble character.

"I ask Your forgiveness for the times my character has not been Christ-like. I determine from now on to let the Word dwell in me until it produces the fruits of love, peace, patience and kindness that I need as a wife and mother.

"Thank You, Lord, for enabling me in this area of my life.

"In Jesus' Name, Amen."

Today's Scripture Reading: Proverbs 31:10-31

Affirmation: "Because of God's Spirit within me, I possess inner beauty and am a wife of noble character."

Affirmation Scriptures: Proverbs 12:4a; 1 Peter 3:1-6.

Week 12 Day 6
Love Your Wife

Husbands, love your wives, just as Christ loved the church and gave himself up for her....In this same way, husbands ought to love their wives as their own bodies. He who loves his wife loves himself.

Ephesians 5:25,28 NIV

Love your wife as Christ loved the Church and gave Himself up for it. What kind of love is this? Forgiving love, unselfish (self-sacrificing) love, unconditional love, redeeming love.

As a husband, perhaps you feel you have a wife who is impossible to love. There are several things you can do to "cure" this situation.

Look into the past and find what it was in your wife that attracted you to her in the first place, the thing that made you want to marry her. Does she still possess that quality or those qualities? If not, could it be *your* inconsideration and selfishness that has caused her to change?

Check yourself. Are you the spiritual leader in your home that you should be? Can your wife look to you, as her head, for direction and guidance that is from God through you?

Do you let your wife know that you love her and appreciate all the work she does to keep your family intact and your home running smoothly? Do you thank her for things such as a clean house, good hot meals or clean clothes? Have you let her know how important she is to you as your wife and as the mother of your children?

Do you tell her, "I love you"? Do you back up those words with thoughtful and caring actions?

If your wife is lacking in some areas, start praising the Father, in faith, for the kind of wife you want. For example: "I praise You, Father, for a wife who loves our children and me and who works diligently to provide a good home for us. I thank You for helping her desire to keep the house clean, to cook nutritious meals, and to provide for our physical needs. I thank You that she is a good sex partner and that we enjoy mutually fulfilling sexual union with each other."

Be sure you are confessing things that *God desires* in your marriage, then you can base your faith on Romans 4:17 — calling "things that are not as though they were."

Of course, marriage is a two-way street; but Biblically you, as the husband, are the head of your home and are to be the spiritual leader. When you get in line with God's will and start doing what His Holy Spirit directs you to do in your marriage relationship, then you will see, through God's power, a resurrection of your marriage that will amaze you! You will look back at the past and wonder if that "hurting marriage" could have ever really been yours!

Prayer: "Father God, I confess to You that I have not always been the husband and head of my home that I should have been. I ask Your forgiveness for my selfishness and inconsideration. I praise You for enabling me to be the head of my home that You would have me be. I bless our home with peace and joy and our relationship with a true spirit of love.

"In Christ's Name, Amen."

Today's Scripture Reading: Ephesians 5:25-33

Affirmation: "I love my wife. She is God's gift to me. I protect her and provide security for her."

Affirmation Scriptures: Ephesians 5:25,28; 1 Peter 3:7; Hebrews 13:4; Proverbs 5:18,19, 12:4, 19:14, 31:10,31.

Week 12 Day 7
A Captivating Marriage

…may you rejoice in the wife of your youth….may you ever be captivated by her love.

Proverbs 5:18,19 NIV

How can you have a captivating marriage that is full of joy, peace, fulfillment, excitement? Many hurting couples would like an answer to that question! I can give you the answer. It is found in God's ways as stated in His Word.

(You may not agree with all of my comments on the scriptures we've used this week. Although I feel the Lord led me as I wrote them, I do not claim to be infallible! But whether you agree or disagree with me personally, you must believe that God's Word is true, otherwise you wouldn't be reading this book each day. So pray that the eyes of your heart — your spiritual understanding — will be open to God's Spirit as you read the verses in the Bible concerning marriage.)

Use the Word of God as the spiritual foundation for your marriage. When the *spirit* of your marriage comes into line with God's ways, you will find that the everyday details will take care of themselves. Eventually they will conform to His ways and your marriage and home will have the good qualities you desire.

Of course, this will work best if both you and your mate are willing to follow God's ways. But, if either partner uses these principles, it will greatly enhance the marriage, because the two of you are "one flesh." (Gen. 2:24.) Also, you and God are definitely a majority when you work together using His Word.

In the Bible, the directions about family life and marriage are mostly directed to the husband or father in the home. Since he is to be the head of the home, this is not surprising. So, husband, if you have a faltering marriage, you are the one who is most apt to be able to see it "healed" by using God's ways. It is a rare wife indeed who will not respond to a husband who is forgiving, unselfish, considerate and loving!

And you, wife, do not despair if your husband isn't a Christian. When you start speaking in faith for his salvation and for the "healing" of your relationship, you will open a very powerful avenue for God to work through.

Prayer (To be prayed together by husband and wife, if possible): **"Father, we come to You in Jesus' Name. We ask You for forgiveness for the sins we have committed against our marriage. We ask that the spirit of love in our relationship be restored and that our marriage become what You intended a Christian home to be.**

"Father, we will take the responsibility of reading Your Word concerning marriage and family life, and will use it as a guide for our home.

"We praise You that Your Spirit will be working in and through us to bring fulfillment and joy to our renewed relationship. If it is not already so, we speak in faith that it will become a reality soon.

"Thank You for Your Word and Your ways, Lord. Help us to follow them completely!

"In Jesus' Name we pray, Amen."

Today's Scripture Reading: Genesis 2:18-24; Colossians 3:18-21

Week 13
Parent-Child Relationships

Week 13 Day 1
Family Relationships: Parent-Child

Reverence for God gives a man deep strength; his children have a place of refuge and security.

Proverbs 14:26 TLB

The responsibility of raising children in today's society is one that sobers almost any parent. We realize we must possess wisdom, strength and self-control. The correct concept of God, "reverence" for Him, will give us this needed strength.

We achieve this right concept of God and relationship with Him through our daily contact with Him in prayer, by studying the Bible and by confessing His Word.

Our security and strength of spirit, based on God's Word, is recognized by our children's spirits (intuitively). They see and know that God is working in us. The spiritual tone of our home provides them with refuge from the world's hurts and rejections.

Security is probably a child's foremost need. True security in the home can be provided only when parents have a correct relationship with God, one which leads to a right and good relationship with each other and with each child.

If you feel you have failed in providing such an atmosphere in your home, you need to ask God to divinely heal you from guilt over past parental inadequacies and failures. You may also need to forgive your children for any hurts, embarrassments, or anger they've caused you. Please pray this prayer for yourself and for each one of your children:

Prayer: "Father, I come to You in the Name of Jesus, Your Son and my Savior. I ask forgiveness for my wrong

attitudes of anger, unforgiveness and hostility toward my children. Forgive me also, Father, for the unkind and harsh words I've spoken to or about them. I repent of the wrong punishments I've used in disciplining them. Thank You, Father, for forgiving me; I accept Your mercy.

"I accept _____ as a child given to me by You, in Your infinite wisdom. I now rebuke and cancel all negative statements I've ever made about _____ in the past. I come against those statements with the energy of Jesus' blood to nullify any negative influence they might have over _____ or me or our family situation. Help me to see _____ with Your eyes of love, to see his/her uniqueness and potential in the same way as You view them. I make a decision of my will to accept and love _____, and to treat him/her with compassion and understanding from this time forward.

"I bless _____ with a spirit of cooperation. I bless him/her with the knowledge that he/she is loved and accepted. I bless him/her with self-confidence and peace. Father, I ask that You, through the healing power of Jesus Christ, heal the past hurt and anger that we have had in our relationship. I say that we are now free to develop a new relationship based on love and compassion, understanding and cooperation.

"In Jesus' Name, Amen."

Today's Scripture Reading: Psalm 127:3-5

Affirmation: "I have God's wisdom and compassion in my relationship with my children."

Affirmation Scriptures: Psalm 112:1,2, 101:2; Proverbs 22:6,15, 23:13,14, 29:17; Ephesians 6:4; Colossians 3:21; Titus 2:4,5; 2 Timothy 1:12.

Week 13 Day 2
God's Promises I

Our children too shall serve him, for they shall hear from us about the wonders of the Lord.

Psalm 22:30 TLB

Here is a promise of God, with as usual, a stipulation to be met in order to make the promise come true — a condition we, as parents, must strive to meet.

First, we will have to be in alignment with God's will so that His power can flow through us to create "wonders of the Lord." We need to see miraculous answers to prayer that we can share with our children.

I suggest a family devotional time in which family members share requests and then the answers to these prayers. Some other "wonders of the Lord" to be shared with children are the wonders found in nature: The beauty of sunsets, flowers and mountains; the unique variety found in foods, animals and in people; the glory and power seen in thunderstorms, quiet starlit nights and the ocean. There is wonder in each day God gives us. We can make our lives richer and fuller by being aware of them and sharing them with our children.

Then there is the wonder of life itself and all the joys that come from simply being alive and being a child of God — the wonder of eternal life and God's plan being fulfilled in and through us as we serve and love Him. All these and more we can share with our children so that they too will be led to love and serve our heavenly Father.

Prayer: "Father, I thank You for the abundance and beauty and wonder of Your world and my life. I ask to be blessed with wisdom and insight so I can effectively share these wonders with my children. I accept Your promise that as I do so, they will be led to serve You and be Your children.
"In Christ's Name, Amen."

Today's Scripture Reading: Psalm 22:26—23:6

Week 13 Day 3
God's Promises II

"All your sons will be taught by the Lord, and great will be your children's peace."

Isaiah 54:13 NIV

How do we, as parents, open the path so our sons (and daughters) will be taught by the Lord? It is through His

Word that the Lord teaches. Therefore we have a very important role to play in assuring that our children see the value of God's Word.

The very best way for our children to be taught the importance of the Word of God is by our example. They need to see that we study and use God's Word daily. Seeing us having daily devotions, hearing us use verses we have memorized as we stand against Satan's attacks, hearing the Word read in our family devotions — all these will help our children see that the Bible has great relevance for their lives too.

Only as our children see us applying the Word and living consistently with peace, love and joy in our lives can we expect them to stand against the temptations of drinking, drugs, pornography, demon-inspired music and the occult.

In the 60s our youth seemed to be determined to "get even" with society and its materialism. They were very destructive to our institutions and negative toward what their parents felt were important values.

In the 70s they saw they hadn't changed society much by all their rebellion against it, so they sought escape through sexual "liberation," drugs, and drinking — many times to the point of self-destruction.

It was a sad commentary on the ineffectiveness of our church programs, our educational system and our social services that the youth of our nation were often (in their own vernacular) "wasted" on drugs.

In the 80s I believe our young people are searching for the supernatural and for peace. Their "solution" seems to be a mixture of yoga, eastern meditation-type religions, the occult and drugs.

The only way to true peace for these misguided young lives is the rebirth of their spirits through accepting Jesus as Savior and making Him Lord in their lives. Then they must grow in this experience by using God's Word as a vital part of their daily lives, renewing their minds.

But we adults *must* accept our responsibility! Recently a Denver newspaper printed an article about rearing children. The question was raised (but never answered): How can we bring up good, moral, caring, responsible children? The answer is, we *can't*! Not unless we, as parents and adults, are willing to change our natures and lifestyles. There is no hope for the younger generation until we become good, moral, caring, responsible (and I would add, *Godly*) examples.

We adults must let God change us first! Notice God's warning to us in Hosea 4:6: "My people are destroyed for lack of knowledge;...*seeing you have forgotten the law of your God, I will also forget your children*" (*AMP*).

Prayer: "Father, today I not only lift up my own children to You but all the searching, disillusioned youth of our world. May Your Holy Spirit work in and through me and all parents and Christian youth workers that we may be spiritually mature, walking in wisdom so these children and youth may see Christ's love and compassion through us. May we be a light to draw them to You — a shining and pure example to them of your love.

"Cleanse all selfishness and anger out of us and bless us with pure love and wise compassion.

"I lift up Jesus as Lord and pray this in His powerful Name, Amen."

Today's Scripture Reading: Proverbs 14:1-35, 15:1-6

Week 13 Day 4
Our Children's Heritage

...happy is the man who delights in doing his (God's) *commands.*

His children shall be honored everywhere, for good men's sons have a special heritage.

Psalm 112:1,2 TLB

Who among us does not want a better life, a better world, for our children and grandchildren? I believe it is a universal desire of parents that their offspring have a happier, more fulfilled life than they themselves have had. Good parents everywhere strive to provide more education and better opportunities for their children, hoping they in turn will have fuller, happier, more productive lives.

But unfortunately, in our counseling we find that unhappy parents with poor home situations produce unhappy children with poor home situations. The problems of unfaithfulness, divorce, alcoholism, and poverty are usually repeated in the homes of the next generation. In fact, when a person comes to us for counseling, one way we go about finding out about his problems, if he is hesitant to admit to them, is simply to ask him about his parents' problems. They are usually the same or quite similar.

And, of course, we find that those people we counsel from stable, happy, Christian homes have much fewer problems; a far greater percentage of them have happy stable marriages and homes.

A key word that we should consider in today's verse is the verb "delights." I spent much of my life in a church in which God's laws were looked upon as a duty and obligation rather than a delight. Condemnation and guilt were heaped upon people from the pulpit to try to keep them in line with church doctrine. This led to unhappiness and rebellion among the teenagers.

I now attend a church where the pastor is delighted with God and preaches His love and caring and a positive Christian lifestyle. The joy and love and non-condemning attitude in our present church is wonderful. It produces a sincere desire to know God rather than to rebel against Him.

Probably our toughest counseling situations are those with people who have been brought up in homes where the "letter of the law" was upheld, but the "spirit of the law" was lacking. Such an atmosphere produces bitterness and buried anger.

As Christian parents, we must show the joy and fulfillment found in following God's ways, rather than upholding strict behavorial standards that are almost impossible to live up to. As we delight in doing God's commands, we will give our children a special heritage.

Prayer: "Father, please teach me how to delight in Your ways. I affirm that I have joy and delight in my life as I follow You. I thank You that this precious heritage will be passed on to my children and they will bring honor to You and to our family.

"In Jesus' Name, Amen."

Today's Scripture Reading: Psalm 112, 113

Affirmation: "I accept my children as a gift from God the Father to me. God's love flows through me to them."

Affirmation Scripture: Psalm 127:3, 101:2; Proverbs 14:26, 29:15,17; Ephesians 4:2; 1 Timothy 3:4; 1 Thessalonians 2:11,12.

Week 13 Day 5
Godly Discipline

Folly is bound up in the heart of a child, but the rod of discipline will drive it far from him.

Proverbs 22:15 NIV

Discipline your son, and he will give you peace; he will bring delight to your soul.

Proverbs 29:17 NIV

God's ways are right. Much of the sorrow which many parents experience because of their children could have been avoided if they had provided them correct, consistent discipline, especially during their formative years. The psychiatrists and psychologists who advised against spanking children were wrong. God's Word shows us the correct way to bring up children.

The Bible does not make mistakes. Thousands of years ago God instructed parents to discipline their children with a rod — to spank them. (Be sure to note that these verses do not say to slap or to beat a child — but to *discipline* him.)

The aim of discipline is to correct wrongdoing and to teach a child self-control. When parents discipline while they are angry and out of control, they do not set the right example before the child. The youngster receives a "double signal." As much as possible, discipline in a calm, matter-

141

of-fact way. Let your child know he is loved and that you are punishing him for his wrongdoing because that is your responsibility as a parent.

It is best to use a "rod" rather than your hand. (Use your hands for soothing and loving your child.) Never slap your child's face! Spank only on his bottom!

If you do sometimes discipline when you are very angry (and what parent hasn't?), ask your child (and God) to forgive you. Do not apologize for the punishment, if it was reasonable and deserved, just ask forgiveness that you did it in anger. (Then as quickly as possible, affirm that you have wisdom and self-control with your children.)

If you are angry, it is best to wait until you are over your anger before administering punishment. Be sensitive to what kind of discipline works best for each individual child. Taking away privileges, sending the child to his room or assigning him work duty are positive alternatives to spanking — especially as the child grows older.

Do your best to be consistent, not letting your child get by with "everything" one day and "nothing" the next! Be very diligent to punish for disobedience. If children do not learn to be obedient to their earthly parents, I believe they will have difficulty being obedient to their heavenly Father when they are older.

Prayer: "Father God, I confess that You are all-wise and rule perfectly. I ask that You bless me with wisdom as I raise my children. Help me to discipline consistently and in a loving way.

"Thank You, Lord, for giving me wisdom so that I will guide my children in Your ways. I bless them with a spirit of cooperation and a desire to be obedient. I thank You that they will bring 'delight to my soul' and honor to your Name.

"In Jesus' Name, Amen."

Today's Scripture Reading: Proverbs 13:20—14:35

Week 13 Day 6
Practical Pointers

Fathers, do not irritate and provoke your children to anger — do not exasperate them to resentment — but rear them [tenderly] in the training and discipline and the counsel and admonition of the Lord.

Ephesians 6:4 AMP

Today's devotional may seem like a list of dos and don'ts, but there are some areas that we, as parents, need to consider to be sure we are not frustrating or "provoking to wrath" (as the *King James Version* puts it) our children.

Childhood should be a time in which children have time to dream, to play, to pursue hobbies. There will be many years of working when they are grown, so let them have time for play now.

I've seen mothers who seemed to do less housework than their children. That is unfair. The keeping of the home is the mother's responsibility. Children should not be expected to spend all day Saturday cleaning house; school is their "job." The time after school and on Saturdays should be mostly their own. It is good for children to have responsibility for a few "chores," but we must be sure we are not putting off onto them the jobs we dislike doing ourselves.

Of course, there are exceptions and differences in families. Children from single-parent homes, from homes in which a parent is ill, or from farm homes must sometimes of necessity be given extra responsibilities. The key here is that children see and know that their parents are working hard too, and not being unfair in what they expect their offspring to do.

Be very sure to keep your word to your children. You would be surprised at the number of adults who are still hurt because an outing or special treat that was promised them in childhood was never provided. If there is a *real* reason the promise can't be fulfilled at the time originally planned, *be sure* to fulfill it as soon as possible — and explain the delay to your child!

If at all possible, take some time each week to do something with your children that they want to do: a picnic, family game time, eating out in a restaurant of their choice. These events don't have to involve a great deal of expense, the main object is that you are together as a family doing something your children have chosen to do. This shows them that you care about them and their desires. (If you have more than one child, rotate who gets to choose from week to week.)

Use common courtesy and kindness with your children. Say please and thank you; try not to embarrass them in public or in front of friends; don't yell at them. Consideration and praise go a long way toward developing a cooperative attitude in children.

The best, most effective way to instruct a child in God's ways is through your own life; being a living example of God's love and righteousness. A parent who walks in God's ways, especially in his or her day-to-day life in the home, is by far the most powerful influence in a child's life.

Family devotions, church attendance, church camps, reading good books, these are all good influences; but your *consistent* walk with Jesus is most important of all!

Prayer: "Lord, I ask Your forgiveness for the sins I've committed against my children and the mistakes I've made in raising them. Help me from now on to walk in Your wisdom and guidance in my family.

"Thank You for the guidelines given in Your Word. Help me to know and use them each day. I ask that Your Holy Spirit enable me to walk in kindness and patience.

"Thank You for my children and the love that we have for each other.

"In Jesus' Name, Amen."

Today's Scripture Reading: Isaiah 44:1-8, 21-26; Colossians 3:21 (AMP)

Week 13 Day 7
Another Promise

Train up a child in the way he should go [and in keeping with his individual gift or bent], and when he is old he will not depart from it.

Proverbs 22:6 AMP

Notice that this verse says, "the way he *should go*," not the way he *shouldn't go*! Many churches and parents are so busy saying, don't smoke, don't drink, don't swear, don't dance, etc., that they forget to teach the child the things he should do. They should be teaching the positive aspects of Christianity: Bible reading, prayer, self-control, obedience, the ways of God's Word.

I like what *The Amplified Bible* added in brackets — that the training should be individualized. Each child is different, that is why we need to confess God's wisdom daily as we guide their lives.

As you train your child by discipline, by word, and, most importantly, by example, God's promise is that he will walk in right ways. What a wonderful reward to have children who love and serve God!

Frequently my own father says how thankful he is to have Christian children (all five of us are serving the Lord) and grandchildren. I know it is a comfort and joy to him to see the fruit in our lives and to know that we pray for him.

If you have children who weren't trained in God's ways and aren't serving Him now, you may feel discouraged (perhaps even guilty) about it. The best thing you can do is be sure you are walking correctly before God, and then pray! Here is a prayer that I believe will open the door for God to work mightily to bring your children to Him:

Prayer: ''Father God, I ask Your forgiveness that I did not always train my children in Your ways. Please forgive my ignorance, mistakes and even sins against them. I ask that the hurts I caused them will be forgiven and released by them and that they will be healed of those hurts and freed from all anger and bitterness.

"I thank You that my children have a thirst for righteousness and a desire to serve You, Lord. I praise You that You are sending loving Christians to witness to them and to show Your love to them. I bind Satan and say that he can no longer blind my children to my love or to Your love.

(If your children are not born again or Spirit-filled, add to your prayer this affirmation based on Romans 4:17.) "I thank You that my children are born again, that they have made Jesus Lord in their lives and are filled with Your Holy Spirit.

"I praise You, Father, that we are all Christians in our family and will enjoy the glory of heaven with You in an unbroken family circle.

"In Jesus' Name, Amen."

Today's Scripture Reading: Matthew 17:14-20, 19:13-15

ORDER FORM

Please send me _____ additional copies of Vol. I
of *IMAGE TO IMAGE* at $5.00 per copy $ _____

Please send me _____ additional copies of Vol. II
of *IMAGE TO IMAGE* at $5.00 per copy $ _____

Please send me Rita's first book, *SET MY
HEART FREE*, at $5.00 per copy $ _____

                              TOTAL ENCLOSED $ _____

Tear out and mail with check or money order to:
    Derin's Coffee Shop®
    P. O. Box 2042
    Windsor, CO 80550

You may use Mastercard _____

        Visa   _____

☐☐☐☐ ☐☐☐ ☐☐☐ ☐☐☐

Expiration date _____